IAN McANDREW
on
POULTRY & GAME

IAN McANDREW
on
POULTRY & GAME

© 1990 The Hamlyn Publishing Group Ltd/
Amazon Publishing Ltd
Text © Ian McAndrew 1990

First published in Great Britain in 1990
by The Hamlyn Publishing Group Ltd/
Amazon Publishing Ltd

ISBN 1 855100 29 0

Printed by Printer Portuguesa, Mem Martins, Portugal

Editor: Jennifer Jones
Art Director: Linda Cole
Designer: Ingrid Mason
Illustrator: Sally Kindberg
Photographer: Martin Brigdale
Stylist: Andrea Lampton
Indexer: Alexandra Corrin

Contents

INTRODUCTION

Poultry, but more especially game, is a subject close to my heart. Why? Well for the last eight years or so I have been, and indeed still am, a keen shooting man. Shooting for sport, I know, is a subject many people find disagreeable, and the anti-bloodsports league is a powerful lobby. Nevertheless, it is a pastime that is becoming more and more popular as years go by and one I hope to continue enjoying for many years to come. Without it not only would a part of our history and culture be lost, but our wildlife would become threatened, wildlife and habitat conservancy a thing of the past, and the countryside turned into even greater areas of wheat and rape deserts. No-one would know the pleasures of the first woodcock or the first English partridge of the season.

Imagine a cold winter's morning: a thin covering of snow, the grey skies heavy with more, ready to discharge their cargo without notice. Pick up the gun, call the dogs and set out across the fields. Silence prevails. In the distance, a handful of pigeons are heading this way. Crouching in the hedgerow I wait for them to come within range. Pigeon terrine, pigeon salad with a few toasted kernels, all the menu ideas running through my head, but to no avail, I've been spotted. Truffle and Bella (my dogs) are worrying a patch of brambles, not too keen on going in. Bella scrambles in, belly flat to the ground. The silence is shattered by an almighty explosion. As I accept the rabbit from Bella, having made a retrieve in great style, Truffle is still trying to get out of the brambles, her long ears anchored to the thorns. That will do for today, time to head home with a rabbit for the pot, a roast, I think, watercress and port this time.

Warm Salad of Teal with Cèpes (see page 110)

Game and poultry always were, from the beginning of time, before battery and intensive farming, an important part of man's diet. Game is a natural food, free from additives, hormones, added water – things that are giving rise to increasing concern. It is also almost fat free. Wild animals, because of the very fact that they are wild, hunting and working for their food, produce very little fat. Poultry too, especially free-range, are also low in fat. It is, however, a sad fact that the majority of poultry sold in supermarkets these days are water-filled junkies. Do not despair – there are good, flavoursome and healthy poultry around, and if more people were to demand flavour and quality a little more often than price, there would be even more of it around. Very dear friends of ours, Neil and Frances, who among other things are quail breeders, also rear guinea fowl, chicken and geese. Their birds have a flavour and quality of a standard I have never found anywhere else. Why can't all breeders come up with a similar product, I can hear Frances say. If it were possible, she says, everyone could cook like you. I only know that some things that masquerade as chickens or ducks, quail or guinea fowl, turkey or capons closely resemble what I can only describe as damp paper, and ought never be allowed the light of day under the broad description of food. In fact, some so little represent the original bird as to make me wonder whether there isn't a new animal, as yet undisclosed to us mere mortals, developed by the food barons, that with a little injection here and there changes its shape to suit our needs. If it says turkey on the label then I suppose it must be!

As before I will preach but one lesson, the words of which shall never change. Buy fresh, never frozen, go for quality, not price. Seek out those suppliers that think like you and use only them. One day the message will get through. We do not all want to be fed on a multitude of man-made hormones and vitamins, especially not second-hand.

Poultry

*The term poultry is applied to all types of domesticated fowl,
whether bred for the table or for its eggs. These include
chicken, duck, goose, turkey and guinea fowl. Poultry has
enjoyed a revival over the past decade or so, thanks in the main
to modern farming methods and the modern trend towards
healthier eating habits with people turning away from the
more traditional red meats. On the whole poultry has a lesser
fat content than other meats and is therefore easier to digest.
Although I cannot condone battery farming, it has made all
types of poultry more accessible, but wherever possible steer
clear of battery farmed produce and try to seek out only
genuine free-range birds. The flavour and texture will be
compensation enough for the higher price paid. There can be
little to better the flavour of a farmyard chicken or duck. I hope
to show you in this section that there is more to do with poultry
than just serving it plain roasted or with the inevitable orange
sauce, nice though they are. All poultry is extremely versatile,
none more so than chicken.*

*When choosing your bird, be careful as it needs to be very fresh.
The flesh should be firm with a fine texture, and there should
not be too much fat, even on ducks. The skin should be white to
pale yellow and dry. The breast bone should be straight and
the breasts broad and the bones pink and bright. A bird that is
not too fresh will quickly show tinges of green around the back
bone, the neck and vent. The breast bone on all young birds
will be pliable at the tip.*

CHICKEN

French: *Volaille* German: *Huhn* Italian: *Pollo*

Chicken is the term used to describe domesticated barnyard fowl and includes everything from the baby chicken, or poussin, through to boiling fowl, or poules. The French tend to refer to chickens by names according to their age: here in Britain, we have a tendency to use the word chicken for all birds, irrespective of age or size. The exceptions are poussin, a bird of 4 to 6 weeks old normally weighing between 350–500g/12–18oz, and capon, a desexed bird weighing between 2–4kg/5–8lb. Castration in a cock is now illegal, so to produce a capon, hormones are implanted into the birds.

The chicken is a direct decendant of the jungle fowl of the Indian sub-continent and has been bred and cross-bred to produce the bird we know today – a far cry from what it was only a few years ago. Once upon a time, as the story goes, chicken was a highly prized, expensive and flavoursome meat. Now, sadly, it has become a factory-produced, tender, and often flavourless bird bearing very little resemblance to its former self, except in shape. It is to my mind important to seek out good quality birds, free-range wherever possible. Forget those frozen blocks in the supermarkets. There is now a great deal of interest in chicken as a healthy (salmonella infections aside), low in calorie, almost fat-free form of food, so now we must look to buy only the best that is offered, not those water-filled, tasteless lumps of paper.

When buying chicken, the breast should be quite plump and firm but pliable, the skin bright and the flesh fine grained and free from bruising. If the bird is whole, the feet should be soft, smooth and pliable, the head and crown should be small, and the eyes bright and full. The best indication of age in a larger bird is the breast bone, which should be pliable at the tip – it becomes hard as the bird ages.

Poached Breast of Chicken with Six Vegetables (see page 13)

BREAST OF CHICKEN WITH A BALLOTINE OF ITS LEG ON A BED OF SAVOY CABBAGE

8 PORTIONS

4 × 900g/2lb fresh chickens
750ml/1¼pt brown chicken
    stock (see page 198)
1 × 115g/4oz chicken breast
    boned, trimmed of fat,
    skinned and chopped
½ tsp salt
1 egg white
300ml/½pt double cream
1 tbsp oil
50g/2oz pistachio nuts, shelled
    and finely chopped
15g/½oz truffle, diced
40g/1½oz unsalted butter
175ml/6floz dry white wine
1 medium savoy cabbage
salt and freshly ground white
    pepper

Method

Remove the legs from the chickens then remove the breasts (see pages 216–17), leaving the skin on and the wing bone clean. Set the breasts to one side. Bone out the legs making sure not to cut through the skin. Reserve the bones. Carefully trim away about two-thirds of the meat. Using a meat hammer, lightly flatten out the remaining meat on the skin. Chill the breasts, flattened legs and leg meat. Make the brown chicken stock (see page 198).

Place the spare chicken breast in a food processor with the salt and process until smooth. Add the egg white and process again. Rub this mixture through a fine sieve into a bowl set over ice. Gradually add three-quarters of the cream, mixing in well and being careful not to overwork the mixture as it will easily separate. Test the mousse for consistency by dropping a teaspoon of the mixture into boiling water. If it is too firm, add a little more cream and test again. Chill until required.

Cut the leg meat into small dice. Heat ½ tablespoon of oil in a frying pan and quickly fry the diced meat until browned. Remove from the pan and allow to cool. Once cold, add to the mousse mixture with the pistachios and truffle. Mix in well.

To make the ballotines, spread out the chicken legs and season lightly. Place 2 teaspoons of the mousse in the centre then fold in the two long sides. Fold the other two sides over – the result should be a short dumpy sausage. Place this on to a sheet of cling film, roll up tightly and tie the ends. Plunge the ballotines into a pan of gently simmering water, cover and simmer gently for 10 minutes. Do not allow the water to boil. Drain then plunge into iced water.

Remove each ballotine from its cling film. Heat the remaining oil in a flameproof shallow dish and, once hot, add 15g/½oz of the butter. Season the breasts and the ballotines, then lay the breasts, skin side down, in the pan along with the ballotines. Place in a hot oven, 220°C/425°F/gas 7, for about 4 minutes or until the skin is golden brown. Turn the breasts and the ballotines over and return to the oven for a further 2–3 minutes. Remove them from the pan and leave to rest in a warm place. Pour off the excess fat, add the white wine and reduce until almost gone. Add the chicken stock and return to the boil, and continue reducing until only about two-thirds remains.

To Serve

Remove the outside leaves from the savoy cabbage and discard. Save 8 large leaves from what is left then shred the remainder as fine as possible. Cut each of the saved leaves into two discarding the central rib. Trim each half into a neat oval shape and blanch in boiling salted water. Keep warm. Heat the remaining butter in a pan. When it just starts to sizzle, add the shredded cabbage, season, cover and cook for about 2 minutes, stirring occasionally.

Cut each breast in half lengthways, but leave joined at one end. Slice each ballotine into 6, discarding the ends. Reheat these in a hot oven for about a minute. Place 2 cabbage leaf halves next to each other in the centre of each plate. Spoon the shredded cabbage on to these. Place a sliced ballotine on to 1 leaf and a breast, with its two halves fanned, on to the other. Strain the sauce through a muslin or fine strainer and pour around.

Note

I find it best to make the ballotines the day before they are needed. It is quite a long job and they need to rest a while after the initial cooking. Once cooked, they will keep perfectly well in the refrigerator, still wrapped in their cling film, for 3–4 days.

POACHED BREAST OF CHICKEN WITH SIX VEGETABLES

Method

Cut the courgette, carrot and potatoes into pieces 5cm/2inches long and 2.5cm/1inch wide. 'Turn' them with a sharp knife into barrel shapes. Cook all of the vegetables, except the tomato, separately in boiling salted water until cooked but still slightly crisp. Refresh these in iced water.

Lightly season the chicken, and place in a saucepan with the chicken stock and white wine. Cover, bring to the boil and simmer gently for 10–12 minutes or until cooked. Remove the chicken from the pan, cover and keep warm. Reduce the cooking liquor over high heat until only about 50ml/2floz remains.

To Serve

Add the cream to the reduced stock, return the vegetables, except the tomato, to the sauce and bring it to the boil. Reduce slightly until it starts to thicken. Drain the vegetables from the sauce and put in the chicken breasts to warm through. Arrange the vegetables around the outside of four serving plates in pairs, including the tomato petals, alternating their colours. Place a chicken breast in the centre of the plates. Strip the leaves from the tarragon sprigs. Add to the sauce and place the pan over very low heat. Gradually whisk in the butter, piece by piece, until all the butter has melted into the sauce. Spoon the sauce over the chicken and the vegetables.

2 PORTIONS
2 chicken breasts, skinned and trimmed of excess fat
1 courgette, peeled
1 carrot, peeled
2 potatoes, peeled
4 shallots, peeled and left whole
4 spring onions, trimmed, white part only
1 tomato, blanched, skinned, quartered and seeded
salt and freshly ground white pepper
200ml/7floz chicken stock (see page 198)
50ml/2floz dry white wine
85ml/3floz double cream
2 sprigs of fresh tarragon
25g/1oz cold unsalted butter, diced

POACHED BREAST OF CHICKEN FILLED WITH A RED PEPPER MOUSSE

5 PORTIONS

6 chicken breasts, trimmed of
  excess fat and skinned
6 red peppers
600ml/1pt chicken stock (see
  page 198)
1 tsp salt
1 egg white
150ml/¼pt dry white wine
450ml/¾pt double cream
2 garlic cloves, roughly
  chopped
5 sprigs of fresh dill, to garnish

Method

Save one of the peppers, remove the seeds from the rest and chop
them roughly. Place in a pan with half the chicken stock and bring to
the boil. Simmer until soft, then blend to a purée. Rub the purée
through a strainer and leave to cool. Remove the seeds from the
reserved pepper and cut into strips about 6.5cm/2½ inches long.
Reserve for the garnish.

Remove the bone from one chicken breast and cut up. Process
in a food processor with the salt until smooth. Add the egg white and
process again. Add three-quarters of the pepper purée and mix in
well. Rub the mousse through a fine sieve into a bowl set over ice.
Test the mousse for consistency by dropping a teaspoon into boiling
water. If the mousse is too firm, add a little more purée and test
again. Lay the remaining chicken breasts on their sides. Make a
horizontal cut through each breast from the wing bone end to form a
pocket. Fill a piping bag with the mousse mixture and carefully pipe
this into each pocket, making sure all the air is expelled. Place the
breasts into a pan and add the remaining chicken stock and the
white wine. Cover with buttered paper and bring to the boil. Reduce
the heat and gently poach for about 10 minutes. Remove the chicken
from the pan, cover and keep warm. Return the stock to high heat
and reduce until only about one-quarter remains. Pour in the cream
and add the chopped garlic, bring back to the boil and reduce until
the sauce starts to thicken. Strain through a fine sieve.

To Serve

Put the chicken breasts in a hot oven for a minute or two to reheat.
Arrange the strips of pepper on the plates in neat piles. Place a
breast, cut in half horizontally and fanned to reveal its centre, on to
each plate and carefully pour the sauce over the top and around the
plate. Finally, garnish with a sprig of dill.

Poached Breast of Chicken Filled with a Red Pepper Mousse

CHICKEN AND SORREL SOUP

4 PORTIONS
115g/4oz fresh sorrel
15g/½oz unsalted butter
600ml/1pt chicken stock (see
    page 198)
5 egg yolks
85ml/3floz double cream
salt and freshly ground white
    pepper

This delicate soup is without doubt my favourite – I'm only sorry I can't claim to have invented it. Great care is needed when cooking this soup, as it relies only on egg yolks for its thickening and any excess heat or cooking time will quickly turn it into scrambled eggs. Once cooked, instead of serving it hot try serving it lightly chilled, perfect for a summer evening. If the stock is good then it will jelly slightly once chilled. When serving it hot, a few small croûtons fried in butter could be sprinkled over the top.

Method

Strip the sorrel leaves of their stalks and wash well. Shred the leaves finely. Melt the butter in a saucepan, add the sorrel and cook slowly until soft – about 2 minutes. Pour in the chicken stock and bring to the boil. Whisk the egg yolks and cream together. Remove the pan from the heat and slowly strain the egg mixture into it, stirring continuously. Return the pan to gentle heat and, stirring continuously, cook the soup until it starts to thicken. It is very important not to let the soup get too hot or it will curdle. Season to taste.

To Serve

Pour the soup into individual soup bowls. Serve the soup immediately as once made, it cannot be reheated.

GRILLED POUSSIN WITH ROASTED DUMPLINGS MADE FROM ITS LEGS AND LIVERS

Method

Remove the legs from the poussins and set to one side. Split the birds down the back, then, using a sharp knife, cut through the carcasses either side of the backbone. Flatten the birds out, then carefully remove the rib bones. Skin the legs and remove the meat from the thighs. Cut away the gall bladder and any green parts from the livers. Make the brown chicken stock with the leg bones (see page 198). Cut the leg meat and livers into dice.

Heat a little of the oil in a frying pan then quickly fry the diced chicken until seared. Remove from the pan then fry the livers. In a clean pan, heat a little more of the oil and gently fry the shallots until they turn transparent. Leave them all to go cold.

Whisk the egg with the cream, add the breadcrumbs and leave until the crumbs have soaked up all of the cream. Pick the leaves from the thyme and stir into the bread mixture (save the stalks for the sauce) along with the livers, meat and the shallots. Season the mixture then divide into 8 equal amounts. Cut the caul into 8 pieces, then wrap each portion in the caul to form 8 small balls.

Place the garlic cloves in a pan of cold water and bring to the boil. Simmer for 1 minute – this will take the harsh flavour out of the garlic. Drain and set aside.

Heat the remaining oil in a pan and, when hot, add about 15g/½oz of the butter. Once sizzling, add the chicken dumplings and garlic, roll them in the hot fat to sear them then place in an oven heated to 230°C/450°F/gas 8 for 10–12 minutes turning them occasionally. After 6 minutes remove the garlic. Keep the dumplings and garlic warm. Coat the poussin with seasoned flour. Melt the remaining butter and brush them with it. Place under a preheated hot grill, skin side down, and grill for about 4 minutes. Turn over and grill for a further 6 minutes, keep warm.

Pour off the fat from the pan, add the white wine and the thyme stalks and reduce until amost gone. Add the chicken stock, return to the boil and simmer until reduced by about one-third. Strain the sauce through a fine sieve or muslin.

To Serve

Return the poussin, dumplings and garlic to the oven for about a minute or so to reheat. Remove the central rib from the spring green leaves, blanch in boiling, salted water for 30 seconds, refresh, then warm them through in the sauce. Place a leaf in the centre of each plate, and a poussin on the top of each leaf. Position 2 dumplings at the point of the breasts then arrange 5 cloves of garlic around this. Spoon the sauce over the garlic and around the chicken.

4 PORTIONS

4 poussins
85g/3oz chicken livers, if the poussin come without them
225ml/8floz brown chicken stock (see page 198)
2 tbsp oil
2 shallots, finely chopped
1 egg
120ml/4floz double cream
85g/3oz fresh breadcrumbs
2–3 sprigs of fresh thyme
salt and freshly ground white pepper
50–85g/2–3oz caul
20 garlic cloves, peeled
40g/1½oz unsalted butter
50g/2oz flour
150ml/¼pt dry white wine
4 spring green leaves (optional)

Grilled Poussin with Roasted Dumplings Made from Its Legs and Livers (see page 17)

ROAST BREAST OF BABY CHICKEN STUDDED WITH TRUFFLES AND SERVED ON CHICKEN GALETTES

4 PORTIONS

4 poussins

16 slices of truffle

salt and freshly ground white
  pepper

½ recipe for panada (see page
  207)

50ml/2floz double cream

a little flour

4 tsp oil

25g/1oz unsalted butter

120ml/4floz dry white wine

350ml/12floz brown chicken
  stock (see page 198)

Method

Remove the legs from the poussins and cut off the parson's nose end
of the carcass. Remove the wish bone. Carefully slide 2 slices of
truffle under the skin of each breast. Season inside and out then
truss the birds (see pages 218–20). Skin the legs and remove all the
meat. Process in a food processor until smooth. Add ½ teaspoon of
salt, a little pepper and the panada. Process until smooth. Rub the
mixture through a sieve into a bowl set over ice. Gradually work in
the cream. Divide the mixture into 8 equal sized balls. Dust the
work surface with a little flour and form each ball into a flat pear
shape, each the size of one poussin breast. Layer them between
sheets of lightly greased greaseproof paper and chill until needed.

Heat half the oil in a roasting pan, add half the butter and
quickly sear the birds on all sides over a high heat, browning them
lightly. Lay each bird on one breast in an oven heated to 230°C/
450°F/gas 8 and roast for 5 minutes. Turn the birds on to the other
breast and cook for a further 5 minutes. Leave to rest in a warm
place for 10 minutes. Pour off the fat from the pan and add the white
wine. Reduce over high heat until almost gone. Pour in the chicken
stock and reduce by just over half. Strain the sauce through a fine
strainer or muslin.

To Serve

Heat the remaining oil and butter in a frying pan, and gently fry the
chicken galettes until golden brown on both sides. Keep warm.
Remove the breasts from the poussin and cut off the wing bones.
Return the breasts and galettes to the oven for about 2 minutes to
reheat. Place 2 galettes, side by side, in the centre of each plate.
Place a breast on each of the galettes and spoon over the sauce.

Poached Breast of Chicken with Roasted Vegetables

Method

Cut each carrot into equal halves across then cut each half in half again lengthways. 'Turn' these into large flat barrel shapes. Repeat the process with the celery and courgettes, leaving the skin on the courgettes.

Heat an ovenproof pan and add 25g/1oz of the butter. Once melted and sizzling, add the carrots and cauliflower, toss well in the hot fat and season lightly. Place in an oven heated to 240°C/475°F/gas 9 for 3 minutes, turning occasionally. Add the remaining vegetables, toss well in the fat and season lightly. Return the pan to the oven for a further 3 minutes. Meanwhile in a separate pan, bring the chicken stock to the boil. Lightly season the chicken breasts and carefully lay them into the stock. Gently simmer the breasts, but do not allow them to boil, for 6 minutes. When the vegetables are cooked they should still be a little crisp. Remove them from the pan and keep warm. (Do not wash the pan as you need it again in a couple of minutes).

When the chicken breasts are cooked, remove them from the stock, pour a little of the stock over them to prevent drying out, then cover and keep warm. Transfer the chicken stock to the vegetable pan and reduce over high heat until just under half remains.

To Serve

Return the vegetables and chicken to the oven for 1 minute to reheat.

Add the lemon juice to the stock to heighten the sauce, remove the pan from the heat and gradually whisk in the remaining butter, piece by piece, until it has all melted. Once the butter has been added, do not reheat the sauce. Pour the sauce through a fine strainer or muslin. Arrange the vegetables alternately around the plates allowing 2 pieces of each vegetable per portion. Place the chicken breasts in the centre of each plate and pour the sauce over and around.

4 PORTIONS

4 chicken breasts, skinned and trimmed of excess fat, with wing bone
2 large carrots
3 stalks celery
2 large courgettes
150g/5oz cold unsalted butter, diced
8 cauliflower florets
8 calabrese florets
600ml/1pt strong chicken stock (see page 198)
salt and freshly ground white pepper
juice of ½ lemon

Breast of Chicken with a Broad Bean and Yoghurt Sauce

Breast of Chicken with a Broad Bean and Yoghurt Sauce

It is very rare for me to say that anything frozen is as good as its fresh equivalent but here is the exception to the rule. Frozen broad beans are not only as good as fresh, but in many cases they can be even better, as they tend to be smaller than the fresh ones and therefore sweeter. Depending on the type of yoghurt used, you may find a touch of lemon juice added to the sauce at the end will help sharpen the sauce.

4 PORTIONS
4 chicken breasts, trimmed of
    excess fat and skinned
salt and freshly ground white
    pepper
300ml/½pt chicken stock (see
    page 198)
120ml/4floz dry white wine
120ml/4floz double cream
275g/10oz frozen broad beans,
    blanched and shelled
12 basil leaves
2 tomatoes, blanched, peeled,
    seeded and diced
3 tbsp natural yoghurt

Method

Lightly season the chicken breasts and place them in a saucepan. Pour over the chicken stock and white wine, cover and simmer gently for 10–12 minutes. Remove from the pan, cover and keep warm. Reduce the stock over high heat until about 85ml/3floz remains.

To Serve

Place the chicken breasts in an oven heated to 200°C/400°F/gas 6 for about 2 minutes to reheat.

Add the cream and the broad beans to the stock, bring to the boil and reduce slightly. Shred the basil leaves and add them to the sauce along with the diced tomato. Over very low heat, stir in the yoghurt. Keep the sauce warm, but once the yoghurt has been added do not allow the sauce to get too hot. Remove the wing bones from the breasts, cut the meat into 6 slices across and at a slight angle. Drain the beans and the tomato from the sauce and form them into an oval nest in the centre of the plates, place a sliced breast in the centre of each and spoon the sauce over and around the chicken.

Breast of Chicken with Redcurrants

This very simple recipe also works well with other types of poultry and game, the sharpness of the currants complementing meats such as pheasant, duck, guinea fowl and even venison. Every year I eagerly await the arrival of the first currants, they are such a versatile, colourful and attractive fruit.

4 PORTIONS

4 chicken breasts, trimmed of
    excess fat and skinned
225g/8oz fresh redcurrants
salt and freshly ground white
    pepper
2 tsp oil
15g/½oz unsalted butter
85ml/3floz dry white wine
350ml/12floz brown chicken or
    veal stock (see page 198 or
    201)

Method

Sort through the redcurrants saving the best 4 bunches for the garnish. Remove all the stalks from the remainder. Save 25g/1oz of the berries for the sauce. Liquidize the remainder. Pass the resulting liquid through a fine strainer to remove the seeds and skins.

Season the chicken breasts. Heat the oil in a frying pan, add the butter and, when it is sizzling, gently fry the chicken breasts skin side down for 5 minutes. Turn over and cook for a further 5 minutes. Remove from the pan and keep warm. Pour off the fat from the pan and add the white wine. Reduce this over high heat until almost gone. Add the redcurrant juice and the stock. Bring to the boil and reduce until the sauce starts to thicken.

To Serve

Cut each chicken breast in two horizontally, starting at the point of the breast but stopping just before the wing bone. Place them in an oven heated to 220°C/425°F/gas 7 to reheat. Strain the sauce through a fine sieve or muslin on to the reserved 25g/1oz currants. Spoon a little of the sauce and the berries on to each plate. Fan the breasts out on to the sauce and spoon the remaining sauce and berries over the chicken. Garnish each plate with a bunch of redcurrants.

BREAST OF CHICKEN WITH ASPARAGUS

Method

Trim the woody ends from the asparagus and peel them. Cook in boiling salted water until tender but crisp. Refresh in iced water. Once cold, cut the tips off so they are about 9cm/3.5 inches long. Cut the rest of the stalks into 1cm/½ inch pieces. Set aside.

Lightly season the chicken breasts, place in a saucepan and add the chicken stock and white wine. Cover the pan and simmer gently for 10–12 minutes. Remove the breasts and keep warm. Add the lemon juice and reduce over high heat until about 85ml/3floz remains.

To Serve

Place the chicken breasts in an oven heated to 200°C/400°F/gas 6 for 2 minutes to reheat. Add the cream to the stock and bring to the boil. Reduce the heat to low and gradually whisk in the butter, saving about 15g/½oz, until all the butter has melted. Add the diced asparagus, tomato and two-thirds of the chervil leaves. Keep the sauce warm. In a small pan, gently heat the asparagus tips in the saved butter; season with a little salt. Place a chicken breast in the centre of each plate and spoon the sauce over and around. Place 4 asparagus tips on top and scatter over the remaining chervil.

4 PORTIONS

4 chicken breasts, trimmed of excess fat and skinned
16 asparagus tips
salt and freshly ground white pepper
300ml/½pt chicken stock (see page 198)
85ml/3floz dry white wine
juice of ¼ lemon
175ml/6floz double cream
85g/3oz cold unsalted butter, diced
2 tomatoes, blanched, skinned, seeded and diced
4 tbsp chervil leaves

BREAST OF CHICKEN WITH FIGS

Method

In a small saucepan, bring the port and the strip of lemon to the boil. Add 2 of the figs and poach for 2 minutes. Remove from the pan and allow to drain and cool. Roughly cut up the remaining 2 figs and add them to the port. Simmer these for about 4 minutes then liquidize.

Lightly season the chicken breasts. Heat the oil in a frying pan with the butter and gently fry the breasts for about 4 minutes each side. Once cooked, remove them from the pan and keep warm. Pour off the fat from the pan and add the fig purée. Reduce by about one-third over a high heat. Pour in the veal stock and reduce by half.

To Serve

Place the chicken breasts in an oven heated to 190°C/375°F/gas 5 for about 2 minutes to reheat. Pour any juices from the chicken into the sauce and return it to the boil. Strain the sauce through muslin and keep warm. Cut each of the poached figs into 8 slices. Arrange 4 slices on to each plate towards the edge. Slice each breast horizontally into two, starting at the point of the breast but stopping just before the wing bone. Fan each breast on to the plates and pour the sauce over and around the breasts.

4 PORTIONS

4 chicken breasts, skinned and trimmed of excess fat
200ml/7floz port
1 strip pared lemon rind
4 fresh ripe figs
salt and freshly ground white pepper
2 tsp oil
15g/½oz unsalted butter
300ml/½pt veal stock (see page 201)

BALLOTINE OF CHICKEN WITH A SALAD OF CHICORY

6 PORTIONS

6 chicken legs
2 tsp oil
40g/1½oz pistachio nuts
½ tsp salt
1 egg white
225ml/8floz double cream
salt and freshly ground white
    pepper
15g/½oz truffle, diced
50ml/2floz white wine vinegar
6 shallots, finely chopped
120ml/4floz olive oil
450g/1lb chicory
2 tsp finely chopped parsley
4 tbsp nut oil

Method

Draw the sinews from each leg. Remove the bone from each leg. Using a sharp knife, carefully pare away about half of the meat from each leg leaving only a thin covering of meat on the skin. Using a meat hammer, lightly bat out the legs and put them to one side. Dice half of the removed meat. Heat the 2 teaspoons of oil in a frying pan, and quickly sear the dice in the hot fat. Drain and allow to go cold. Blanch the pistachio nuts in boiling salted water and leave to go cold. Skin them, then roughly chop.

Process the remaining meat and ½ teaspoon of salt in a food processor until smooth. Add the egg white and process until it stiffens. Rub this mixture through a sieve into a bowl set over ice. Gradually add three-quarters of the cream, mixing it in well each time before adding more. Test the consistency of the mousse by dropping a teaspoon of the mixture into boiling water. If it is too firm, add a little more cream and test again. Lightly season the diced chicken and add to the mousse with the truffle and pistachio nuts. Spread out each chicken leg and season lightly. Divide the mousse mixture between them. Roll each leg around the mousse to form a large sausage shape, making sure that the mousse is totally enclosed. Wrap each leg tightly in cling film and twist the ends. Drop the ballotines into a pan of boiling water and simmer very gently for 20 minutes. Leave to cool in the water. Drain and chill for at least 3 hours.

Bring the vinegar to the boil, add the shallots and return to the boil. As soon as it comes to the boil remove from the heat and leave to go cold. Season and whisk in the olive oil.

To Serve

Trim any outside leaves from the chicory and remove the core. Slice the leaves thinly, add the chopped parsley, season lightly then mix in the nut oil. Place a 10cm/4 inch pastry cutter in the centre of each plate and divide the chicory between them, forming it into a flat mound. Remove the cling film from the ballotines and slice each one into 8 or 10 slices. Arrange the slices in a circle on the top of the chicory. Spoon the vinaigrette around the chicory and remove the pastry cutters.

FRICASSEE OF CHICKEN AND CLAMS WITH MORELS

If you use dried morels for this recipe, they must be soaked in cold water for at least 2 hours before using to bring them back to their original state. Dried are, however, not as good as fresh: their flavour is a lot stronger and therefore you should reduce the quantity. Fresh morels will probably prove quite difficult to get but are well worth the effort. When buying clams or any molluscs, make sure they are still alive; the shells should be tightly closed or they should snap shut as soon as they are handled. Alternatively, canned ones will do just as well. Rinse these before adding to the sauce as they are packed in brine and this will oversalt the finished sauce. Cockles can be used to achieve the same result.

4 PORTIONS

4 chicken breasts, skinned, boned and trimmed of excess fat

900g/2lb fresh clams in their shells

1 tbsp oil

85g/3oz white mirepoix (onion, leek, celery)

150ml/¼pt dry white wine

150ml/¼pt fish stock (see page 199)

1 tsp white peppercorns

115g/4oz fresh morels or 25g/1oz dried

salt and freshly ground white pepper

25g/1oz unsalted butter

50ml/2floz dry sherry

300ml/½pt double cream

sprigs of fresh dill, to garnish

Method

Clean the clams thoroughly and leave to soak in fresh water for about 15 minutes. Change the water and leave for a further 15 minutes. Repeat the process once more. Heat the oil in a pan with a tight fitting lid and sweat the vegetables, without colouring, until they start to soften. Add the wine and stock and bring to the boil. Add the clams and peppercorns, cover with the lid and cook until the clams open – about 5–8 minutes. When cooked, drain the clams and save the liquor. Once cold, remove them from their shells and set aside.

Remove the fillets from the chicken breasts and, angling the knife slightly, cut each fillet into four. Cut each breast into 2 lengthways, then cut each strip through at an angle to get about 5 pieces out of each.

If using fresh morels, discard the stalks and, if the caps are too large, cut them into pieces. If they are small, just cut them in half – you will find that the caps are hollow and unless they are cut in half the dirt cannot be removed. Brush off any dirt.

Season the pieces of chicken. Heat the butter in a frying pan until it starts to sizzle, and sear the chicken in the hot butter. Remove them from the pan and pour off the fat. Add the sherry and reduce until almost nothing is left. Add 300ml/½pt of the reserved clam cooking liquor and reduce by three-quarters. Add the cream, bring back to the boil again and reduce until it starts to thicken. Add the pieces of chicken and allow to simmer over very low heat until cooked – about 5 minutes.

To Serve

When ready to serve, add the morels and the clams to the sauce and allow to warm through gently for about 1 minute. Divide the chicken and clams out equally between plates or bowls, pour over the sauce and garnish with the sprigs of fresh dill.

Fricassee of Chicken and Lobster with Spring Vegetables

4 PORTIONS

4 × 115g/4oz chicken breasts, skinned, boned and trimmed of excess fat

1 × 675g/1½lb live lobster

2.25l/4pt court bouillon (see page 201)

8 small carrots

8 small turnips

12 mangetout

12 small French beans

8 small heads calabrese

1 tbsp oil

25g/1oz unsalted butter

salt and freshly ground white pepper

120ml/4floz brandy

85ml/3floz dry sherry

350ml/12floz lobster sauce (see page 204)

300ml/½pt double cream

sprigs of fresh dill or chervil, to garnish

Method

Bring the court bouillon to the boil, plunge in the lobster and poach for 4–5 minutes. Allow to cool in the liquor. When cold, remove the meat from the shell. Cut each claw into half lengthways and cut the tail meat across into 12 slices.

Cut the chicken breast into 5mm/¼ inch slivers. Peel the carrots and turnips to retain their natural shapes, and top and tail the mangetout and the beans. Break the calabrese into small florets. Blanch them all in boiling salted water for a few seconds and then refresh in iced water.

Heat the oil in a frying pan and, when hot, add half the butter. Season the chicken and quickly sear in the fat without colouring. Remove from the pan. Pour off the fat, add the brandy and the sherry to the pan and reduce until the liquid has almost gone. Pour in the lobster sauce, bring to the boil and reduce a little. Add the cream and return to the boil. Allow the sauce to reduce slightly until it just starts to thicken, then return the chicken to the pan and simmer until the chicken is cooked, about 2 minutes.

To Serve

Add the lobster to the sauce and let it sit over a very gentle heat for a couple of minutes to let the lobster heat through. Do not allow the sauce to boil at this stage. In the meantime, gently reheat the vegetables by tossing them in the remaining butter in a frying pan over low heat. Season them if necessary. When ready, divide the chicken and lobster between bowls, pour over the sauce and sprinkle the vegetables on top. Crown it all with a few sprigs of chervil or dill.

Note

You could of course go quite mad, say hang the expense, and sprinkle a little black truffle cut into fine strips over each dish.

CHICKEN AND LOBSTER 'SAUSAGE' SERVED HOT ON A CREAMY SPRING ONION SAUCE

Method

To make the mousseline, chop the chicken breasts into small pieces, place in a blender or food processor with the ½ teaspoon of salt, and blend to a smooth paste. Add the egg white and process again until it stiffens. Rub the mixture through a sieve into a bowl set over crushed ice. Gradually add two-thirds of the cream, mix in well, then add the sherry and season with a little salt and pepper. Test the mousse by dropping a teaspoon of the mixture into boiling water, and, if it is too rubbery in texture, add a little more cream and test again. Chill until needed.

Bring the court bouillon to the boil, plunge the lobster in, bring back to the boil and continue boiling for 2 minutes. Remove the pan from the heat and allow the lobster to cool in the stock. When it is cold, remove the lobster meat from its shell and cut the meat into 5mm/¼ inch dice. Fold the lobster and chives into the mousseline. Using cling film as a sausage skin, form the mixture into 8 individual sausages and twist the ends. Leave to rest in the refrigerator until needed; they will keep for about 4 hours.

To make the sauce, melt the butter in a saucepan, add the spring onions, season, cover with a lid and sweat until cooked – about 3–4 minutes. Spoon the cooked onions into a food processor and process so that they are just chopped. Return them to the saucepan, stir in the cream and reheat.

To Serve

Drop the sausages, still in their cling film skin, into boiling water and poach for 10 minutes. When cooked, gently remove the cling film. Heat the oil and the butter in a frying pan, and gently roll the sausages in the fat until brown. Place a spoonful of the sauce in the middle of each plate and sit a sausage on top. Garnish with a few sprigs of dill.

Note

The sausages can be cooked up to 3 days in advance and kept in the refrigerator until needed. After poaching, drop the sausages into iced water to cool them rapidly, then store in the refrigerator. To reheat, drop into boiling water and simmer for 2–3 minutes.

MAKES 9 × 85G/3OZ SAUSAGES

2 × 175g/6oz chicken breasts, skinned, boned and trimmed of excess fat
1 × 675g/1½lb live lobster
½ tsp salt
1 egg white
300ml/½pt double cream
1 tbsp dry sherry
salt and freshly ground pepper
1.7l/3pt court bouillon (see page 201)
15g/½oz chopped fresh chives
25g/1oz unsalted butter
2 bunches spring onions, roughly chopped
150ml/¼pt double cream
2 tsp oil
25g/1oz unsalted butter
sprigs of fresh dill, to garnish

DUCK

French: *Canard* German: *Ente* Italian: *Anitra*

Duck is probably the most universally praised member of the poultry family. The term 'duck', like that of chicken, covers many different types and qualities. Obviously originating from the wild duck (see chapter on feathered game, pages 107–18), it is now bred worldwide. In Britain we have always considered the Aylesbury duck to be the finest, whereas in France they prefer the Rouen, Nantes and Barbary, and in America the Long Island is held in great esteem. Great care is needed when buying a duck. At first sight a well presented duck may appear very large and meaty, but on closer inspection it will have a very thick layer of fat under the skin and very little meat. This is certainly the case with the Aylesbury, but not so much for the other breeds. Personally, I do tend to steer clear of our homebred ducks for this very reason, often finding that to get two good one portion-sized supremes, I need to buy a bird weighing about 3.5kg/8lb. Try the French breeds: for the same meat yield as a large Aylesbury, you will only need a 2.25kg/5lb Barbary or Rouen. The British ducks seem to have a much larger and heavier carcass than their French rivals.

Ducks are at their best up to 6 months old. If buying an Aylesbury, then test it for fat covering by pinching the skin along the breast just behind the legs. This will show how much fat the bird is carrying. The end of the breast bone will always be pliable in a young bird and is the best test of age. Alternatively, check the windpipe – if it too is pliable the bird is young, if hard then find another bird.

Breast of Duck Poached in Consommé with Baby Vegetables (see page 33)

Terrine of Duck, Garlic and Herbs

At first sight the amount of garlic used in this terrine may seem a little excessive but if you think about how many portions it serves, and how the garlic is cooked, you will find that it really is not that much at all. I tend to serve this terrine with a salad of 'Cauliflower à la Grecque', scattered with fresh herbs, but any vegetable or mixture of vegetables will do just as well. As with most terrines, forward planning is essential – this one takes two days to make and I think it best eaten no sooner than the day after making, three days in all.

ABOUT 20 PORTIONS
24 duck legs (or 1.5kg/3½lb meat)
1 tbsp salt
2 tbsp water
115g/4oz clarified butter (see page 208)
2 sprigs of fresh rosemary
2 bay leaves
2 sprigs of fresh thyme
few parsley stalks
1 tsp black peppercorns
24 garlic cloves, peeled
115g/4oz mixed fresh herbs
6 large carrots, peeled, blanched and sliced lengthways

Method

Bone out the duck legs. Remove all of the skin and fat, cut into small pieces and set to one side. Cut the meat into 2.5cm/1 inch cubes. Sprinkle the meat with the salt and allow it to stand overnight.

Next day, mix the skin and fat with the water. Process in a food processor until finely chopped. Melt this over low heat and simmer for about 1 hour or until the fat is clear. Once rendered, pour the fat through a fine strainer. Place the leg meat in a pan and pour over the fat. Melt the butter and add this as well. The meat should be just covered with fat – if not then add more butter until it is. Tie the rosemary, bay leaves, thyme, parsley stalks and the peppercorns in a muslin bag and add this to the fat. Place the garlic in a pan of cold water, bring to the boil and simmer for 1 minute (this will take the harsh flavour out of the garlic). Tie the cloves in muslin as with the herbs and add this to the fat also. Place the pan in a roasting pan half-filled with boiling water. Simmer for 2–3 hours on top of the stove. Add more water if necessary. After 1 hour remove the bag of garlic, remove the cloves from the muslin and put to one side.

Once the duck is cooked, remove the bag of herbs and discard. Strain the meat from the fat. Allow the fat to settle for a few minutes then skim off the fat leaving the duck juice behind. There will be anything up to about 600ml/1pt of this. Reduce this juice over high heat until only about a quarter remains. Add to the duck meat along with 300ml/½pt of the fat. Mix it in well and allow to go cold at room temperature.

Finely chop the mixed fresh herbs and, once the duck mixture has gone cold, stir these in. Lightly grease a 28cm/11 inch terrine mould with some of the remaining fat. Dry off the slices of carrot and carefully line the mould with some of these, brushing each slice with a little of the remaining fat. Place in the refrigerator and allow to set.

Press half of the duck mixture into the terrine, making sure there are no air pockets. Lay the cloves of garlic in two rows down the length of the terrine. Place the terrine in the refrigerator for about 20 minutes to set. Once set, press the remaining duck into the terrine.

Return it to the refrigerator and set. Trim the remaining carrot neatly to the top of the terrine and pour on a little of the remaining fat to form a seal. Chill to set.

To Serve

Dip the base of the terrine in hot water for a few seconds. Place a serving plate over the top and invert. Gently tap the ends and it should easily fall out. Cut into slices about 1cm/½ inch thick and serve with the salad of your choice.

BREAST OF DUCK POACHED IN CONSOMMÉ WITH BABY VEGETABLES

Method

Prepare all of the vegetables, retaining their natural shapes where possible. Blanch each vegetable separately in boiling salted water and refresh in iced water. Drain and set to one side. Bring the consommé to the boil in a saucepan large enough to hold the duck breasts. Lightly season each breast and lower into the consommé. Simmer gently for about 8 minutes. Remove from the pan, cover and keep warm. Reduce the consommé by just over half.

To Serve

Return the breasts to the consommé and allow to warm through. Remove them and slice each breast into 6 or 7 slices across and at a slight angle. Place the vegetables in the consommé to reheat while dressing the duck. Arrange the duck slices on the plates in a circle. Drain the vegetables and scatter these over and around the duck. Strain the consommé through muslin and pour it on to the plates over the duck and the vegetables. Scatter the chervil over the top.

4 PORTIONS

4 duck breasts, trimmed of
  excess fat and skinned, with
  bone
8 baby carrots, with their tops
  on
8 baby turnips, with their tops
  on
8 pencil-thin leeks
8 baby courgettes
50g/2oz shelled peas or French
  beans
450ml/¾pt duck consommé
  (see page 42 – omit beetroot)
salt and freshly ground white
  pepper
sprigs of fresh chervil

Confit of Duck with a Salad of Red Cabbage

CONFIT OF DUCK WITH A SALAD OF RED CABBAGE

Confit is one of the oldest classical recipes of all time. Normally made with goose (see page 48), any fatty meat can be treated the same way. Also it would normally be left on the bone whereas here I remove the bones to aid presentation. Before the refrigerator was invented, dishes like this were cooked as a way of preserving food; sealed in its fat in a stone jar, it will keep for months. Served here with a salad of marinated red cabbage (which will also keep for a long time), it gives the dish a glorious splash of colour.

4 PORTIONS
4 duck legs
1 tbsp salt
2 tsp whole white peppercorns, crushed
2 garlic cloves, roughly chopped
2 sprigs of fresh thyme
about 450g/1lb lard or duck fat
300ml/½pt water
1 small red cabbage, weighing about 450g/1lb
1 small onion
salt and freshly ground white pepper
4 tbsp walnut oil
3 tbsp salad oil
5 tbsp sherry vinegar
2 tsp sugar

Method

Bone out the duck legs and save the bones. Lay the boned legs out meat side up and sprinkle with 1 tablespoon of salt. Place in the refrigerator for 24 hours.

After this time, wipe off any excess salt, roll up the duck legs and tie them securely with string. Tie the peppercorns, garlic and thyme in a little muslin to make a bag. Melt the lard or duck fat in a pan and add the muslin bag and duck legs, making sure they are completely covered in the fat. Place the pan in a bain-marie filled with boiling water and cook for 2 hours. Add more boiling water as necessary.

Remove the legs from the pan and place in a dish and keep warm. Remove the muslin bag and discard. Carefully pour the fat over the legs and leave to go cold, preferably overnight. Once the fat is poured over the legs you should be left with about 150ml/¼pt of duck juice. Make a little sauce from this by roughly chopping the saved bones and browning them quickly over high heat. Add the bones to the duck juices with the water. Simmer gently for about 1 hour, skimming as necessary. Strain through muslin.

To prepare the red cabbage, first cut it into quarters, remove the core and very finely chop the leaves. Peel and cut the onion into quarters as well and finely slice. Mix the cabbage and onion together, season, add all the remaining ingredients and mix in thoroughly. Leave to stand for at least 24 hours.

To Serve

Very gently warm the confit through in an oven heated to 180°C/350°F/gas 4. The fat should just be melted – it should not be allowed to get hot! Remove the string from the legs. Cut each leg into 10 or 12 slices. Gently warm the duck sauce again. Place a pile of red cabbage in the centre of each plate. Arrange the duck slices in a circle around the edge of this. Spoon a little of the fat over the duck slices allowing a little to run on to the plate in a circle around the duck. Then spoon a little of the duck sauce over the meat allowing this to run into the fat.

Magret of Duck with Roasted Shallots and a Broad Bean Purée

4 PORTIONS

4 magret breasts, trimmed of
  excess fat
450g/1lb frozen broad beans,
  blanched and shelled
85ml/3floz chicken stock (see
  page 198)
20 shallots
2 tsp oil
40g/1½oz butter
salt and freshly ground white
  pepper
175ml/6floz red wine
450ml/¾pt duck stock (see
  page 199)
25ml/1floz double cream
sprigs of fresh fennel or
  chervil, to garnish

Method

Place the shelled broad beans in a food processor with the chicken stock. Process until quite smooth. If a few lumps still remain then rub the purée through a sieve. Peel the shallots being careful to keep the root end intact.

Heat the oil in a roasting pan and, when hot, add half the butter. Season both sides of each breast. When the butter is sizzling, fry the breasts, meat side down, until browned slightly. Turn the breasts over, place in an oven heated to 240°C/475°F/gas 9 and cook for about 10–12 minutes. When cooked the meat should still be a little pink. Remove from the pan and keep warm.

Pour off the fat from the pan and return to the heat. Add the remaining butter and the shallots, roll these in the butter and season with a little salt. Place the pan in the oven for about 4 minutes, stirring the shallots occasionally to prevent burning. Once cooked, remove them from the pan and keep warm. Pour off the fat. Add the red wine and reduce over high heat until it has almost gone. Add the duck stock and continue reducing until it starts to thicken. Strain the sauce through a fine strainer or muslin.

To Serve

Return the duck breasts and shallots to the oven for about 1 minute to reheat.

Reheat the broad bean purée in a pan with the cream and a little seasoning if necessary. Place 5 shallots in a circle towards the edge of each plate. Pour the sauce on to the plates. Slice each duck breast into 6 slices lengthways and arrange these in the centre of the plates. Spoon a ribbon of broad bean purée in a circle around the sliced duck. It's nice to top each shallot with a sprig of fennel or chervil.

Note

It is quite acceptable to use frozen broad beans. Frozen food is not something I would normally recommend but in the case of broad beans I do find them perfectly good.

Breast of Duck with Raspberries

Method

Score the skin of each breast 6 times lengthways to allow excess fat to drain off during cooking. Purée 175g/6oz of the raspberries in a food processor then rub through a fine sieve to remove the seeds. Save the remaining raspberries for garnish. Heat the oil in a roasting pan, then add the butter. Lightly season both sides of the duck breasts. When the butter is sizzling, add the breasts, meat side down, and sear until they start to brown. Turn over and cook in an oven heated to 240°C/475°F/gas 9 for 10–12 minutes. When cooked they should still be slightly pink. Remove from the pan and keep warm. Pour off the fat, place the pan over high heat and add the vinegar. Reduce until it has evaporated. Add the duck stock and the raspberry purée and reduce until it starts to thicken. Strain the sauce through a fine strainer or muslin and add a pinch of sugar to the sauce, just enough to take away a little of the sharpness.

To Serve

Return the duck breasts to the oven for 1 minute to reheat.

Arrange the reserved raspberries attractively in a pile on each plate. Pour the sauce on to the plates. Remove the wing bones from the breasts, and carve each breast into 6 or 7 slices across and at an angle. Slightly fan each breast out on to the sauce.

4 PORTIONS

4 duck breasts, trimmed of
    excess fat, with wing bones
225g/8oz raspberries
2 tsp oil
15g/1oz unsalted butter
salt and freshly ground white
    pepper
25ml/1floz raspberry vinegar
450ml/¾pt duck stock (see
    page 199)
pinch of sugar

Breast of Duck with Blackcurrant Sauce

Method

Using a sharp knife, score the skin of each duck breast about six times lengthways – this will allow the excess fat from the skin to escape. Remove the currants from their stalks and set to one side.

Heat the oil in a roasting pan then add the butter. Lightly season the duck breasts on both sides. When the butter is sizzling, add the breasts, meat side down and sear them in the hot fat until they have started to brown. Turn over and place in an oven heated to 240°F/475°F/gas 9 for about 10–12 minutes. When cooked, they should still be slightly pink. Remove and keep warm. Pour off the fat, add the white wine and reduce over high heat until almost gone. Pour in the duck stock and the cassis and reduce by half.

To Serve

Return the breasts of duck to the oven to reheat for about 1 minute. Strain the sauce through a fine strainer or muslin on to the blackcurrants. Remove the wing bone from the breasts and carve each breast into 6 or 7 slices. Spoon a little of the sauce on to each plate along with a few of the currants. Fan each duck breast on to this sauce, then spoon the rest of the sauce over the sliced duck.

4 PORTIONS

4 duck breasts, trimmed of
  excess fat, with wing bone
85g/3oz blackcurrants
2 tsp oil
15g/½ oz unsalted butter
salt and freshly ground white
  pepper
50ml/2floz dry white wine
450ml/¾pt duck stock (see
  page 199)
40ml/1½floz crème de cassis

Breast of Duck with a Shallot and Port 'Marmalade'

Method

Place the shallots in a saucepan with the port and the veal stock and bring to the boil. Simmer for 1½ hours. At the end of this time the marmalade should have reduced by at least two-thirds.

Heat the oil with the butter in a roasting pan. Lightly season the duck breasts. Sear the duck breasts on the meat side over high heat until lightly browned. Turn the breasts on to the skin side and transfer them to an oven heated to 230°C/450°F/gas 8 for about 10 minutes. When they are cooked the skin should be crisp and the meat slightly pink. Transfer to a warm place to rest. Pour off the fat from the pan and add the red wine. Reduce over high heat until almost gone, then pour in the duck stock and reduce by one-third.

To Serve

Reheat the duck breasts in the oven for 1 minute. Pour the sauce through muslin. Reheat the marmalade and divide between the plates in piles, just off centre. Slice each duck breast into 6 or 7 slices lengthways, pour the sauce around the marmalade and fan the duck half on to the marmalade and half on to the sauce.

4 PORTIONS

4 duck breasts, trimmed of
  excess fat
225g/8oz shallots, thinly sliced
350ml/12floz port
120ml/4floz veal stock (see
  page 201)
2 tsp oil
15g/½oz unsalted butter
salt and freshly ground white
  pepper
120ml/4floz red wine
300ml/½pt duck stock (see
  page 199)

Breast of Duck on a Bed of Caramelized Apples

Method

Using the point of a sharp knife, score the skin of each breast about six times lengthways – this will allow the excess fat from the skin to escape.

Heat the oil in a roasting pan then add 15g/½oz of the butter. Lightly season the duck breasts on both sides. When the butter is sizzling, add the breasts, meat side down and sear them in the hot fat until they have started to brown. Turn over and place in an oven heated to 240°C/475°F/gas 9 for about 10–12 minutes. When cooked, they should still be slightly pink. Remove the cooked breasts from the pan and keep warm.

Pour off the fat, add the calvados and reduce over high heat until almost gone. Pour in the duck stock and reduce by half. Strain the sauce through a fine strainer or muslin.

To Serve

Cut each apple quarter into 4 slices. Heat the remaining butter in a frying pan, add the apple slices and the sugar and toss well. Fry over high heat until the apple slices are golden brown. Return the duck breasts to the oven for about 1 minute to reheat. Remove the wing bone from each duck breast and carve into 6 or 7 slices lengthways. Arrange the apples into neat piles in the centre of each plate, and pour the sauce on to the plates. Fan each duck breast and place on top of each pile of apples.

4 PORTIONS

4 duck breasts, trimmed of
  excess fat, with wing bone
2 tsp oil
40g/1½oz unsalted butter
salt and freshly ground white
  pepper
50ml/2floz calvados
450ml/¾pt duck stock (see
  page 199)
2 dessert apples, peeled,
  quartered and cored
1½ tbsp sugar

Breast of Duck with a Foie Gras and Herb Butter Sauce

4 PORTIONS

4 duck breasts, trimmed of
    excess fat, with wing bones
65g/2½oz foie gras
85g/3oz unsalted butter
2 tsp oil
salt and freshly ground white
    pepper
25ml/1floz white wine vinegar
300ml/½pt chicken stock (see
    page 198)
20g/¾oz mixed chopped fresh
    herbs (tarragon, chervil,
    dill, chives)

Method

Allow the foie gras and 65g/2½oz of the butter to soften slightly at room temperature, then push the foie gras through a fine sieve. Mix it well with the soft butter and chill. Score the skin of each duck breast about 6 times lengthways to allow the excess fat to drain off during cooking.

Heat the oil in a roasting pan and add the remaining butter to the pan. Lightly season both sides of each breast. When the butter is sizzling, add the duck breasts, meat side down. Sear the breasts over a high heat until lightly browned. Turn over and cook in an oven heated to 240°C/475°F/gas 9 for 10–12 minutes. When cooked the meat should still be slightly pink. Remove from the pan and leave in a warm place. Pour off the fat, add the vinegar and reduce over high heat until gone. Pour in the chicken stock and reduce this over a high heat by two-thirds.

To Serve

Return the duck breasts to the oven for about 1 minute to reheat.

Over very low heat, gradually whisk the chilled foie gras butter in to the sauce, until it has all melted. Add the herbs and allow this to sit for a few seconds for the herbs to infuse. Remove the wing bones from the breasts and carve each breast into 6 or 7 slices lengthways. Divide the sauce between the plates, fan a duck breast on to each plate and serve.

CARAMELIZED BREAST OF DUCK WITH ITS JUICES FLAVOURED WITH LIME AND GINGER

Method

Remove the peel from the limes and cut it into fine julienne strips. Blanch in boiling water for about 10 seconds then refresh in cold water. Segment the limes and save the juice. Peel the ginger, saving the peel, and cut the root into 2.5cm/1 inch batons. Using a sharp pointed knife, score the skin on the duck breasts, making incisions down the length of the breast just to the depth of the fat, in all, about 6 cuts. Doing this will firstly help some of the fat to run away, and secondly allow the sugar to get into the skin. Once scored, lightly season the skin with freshly ground pepper then rub the sugar into the skin. Lightly salt the meat side.

Heat the oil in a pan, add the butter and, when it sizzles, add the duck breasts to the pan, meat side down, and sear them for 1 minute. Turn on to the skin and cook in an oven heated to 230°C/450°F/gas 8 for about 8 minutes. When cooked the duck should still be a little pink. Remove from the pan and leave to rest in a warm place. Pour off the fat from the pan. Return the pan to a high heat and add the wine and lime juice. Reduce this until it has almost gone. Add the stock and the ginger peelings. Return the sauce to the boil, lower the heat and reduce slowly until it starts to thicken slightly.

To Serve

Return the duck breasts to the oven for about 1 minute to reheat.

Place the lime segments in the oven for a few seconds to just warm through. Pour the sauce through a fine strainer or muslin and add about half of the lime julienne and all of the ginger. Leave to stand for 1 minute to infuse. Slice each breast into about 8 slices across and at a slight angle. Spoon some of sauce and its garnish on to the plates and arrange the sliced duck in a circle. Sprinkle the lime segments over and pour on the remaining sauce. Finish the dish by sprinkling over the remaining lime julienne.

4 PORTIONS
4 duck breasts
2 limes
25g/1oz fresh root ginger
salt and freshly ground white pepper
50g/2oz sugar
2 tsp oil
15g/½oz unsalted butter
175ml/6floz dry white wine
225ml/8floz duck stock (see page 199)

Jellied Duck and Beetroot Consommé Topped with Salmon Caviar

4 PORTIONS
1 duck leg
1 stalk celery
½ small onion
1 small leek
1 tomato, blanched, skinned
    and seeded
1 tbsp chopped fresh thyme
225g/8oz beetroot
2 egg whites
1l/1¾pt duck stock (see page
    199)
salt and freshly ground white
    pepper
4 tsp soured cream
50g/2oz salmon caviar
fresh chervil leaves

Method

Skin and bone the duck leg and very finely chop the meat. Finely dice the celery, onion, leek and tomato. Combine these with the chopped meat and thyme in a saucepan. Peel the beetroot, cut a quarter of it into strips about 2.5cm/1 inch long and 3mm/⅛ inch wide. Finely dice the remaining beetroot and add it to the meat and vegetables. Add the egg whites and mix together well. Stir in the cold stock, check the mixture for seasoning and add salt and pepper as required.

Place over high heat, stirring continuously until it almost comes to the boil. Just as it comes to the boil, reduce the heat so that it just simmers. Continue simmering for 30 minutes. Strain the finished consommé through muslin. If there is a thin film of fat on the top of the consommé, this can be removed by pulling a sheet of kitchen paper over the surface.

Boil the beetroot batons in a little of the consommé. When cooked, remove them and drain. Return the consommé to the rest and leave to go cold. Once cold, chill in the refrigerator for about 6 hours, after which time it should have lightly set.

To Serve

Spoon the jellied consommé into serving cups and place a teaspoon of soured cream in the centre. Top with a spoonful of caviar. Sprinkle a few beetroot batons over this then scatter the chervil leaves over the top.

Note

If the duck stock is jelly before making the consommé then it will jelly again. If it was not, then two leaves of gelatine added while the consommé is still hot will ensure it setting. Do not serve the consommé directly from the refrigerator but allow to come to room temperature.

Jellied Duck and Beetroot Consommé Topped with Salmon Caviar

BREAST OF DUCK WITH GREEN PEPPERCORNS

4 PORTIONS

4 duck breasts

1 stalk celery

1 carrot

1 turnip

2 tsp oil

25g/1oz unsalted butter

salt and freshly ground white
    pepper

85ml/3floz cognac

350ml/12floz duck stock (see
    page 199)

25g/1oz green peppercorns

Method

Trim the duck to remove any excess fat and sinew. Peel the vegetables then cut them into neat 2.5 cm × 6 mm/1 × ¼ inch batons. Blanch in boiling salted water for about 1 minute so they are still a little crisp. Refresh in iced water.

Heat the oil with half the butter in an ovenproof pan. Lightly season both skin and meat sides of the duck breasts, place them in to the pan, meat side down, and sear over high heat until lightly browned. Turn on to their skin side and roast in an oven heated to 230°C/450°F/gas 8 for 10–12 minutes. Once cooked, the meat should still be slightly pink in the centre. Remove the breasts from the pan and keep them in a warm place to rest. Pour off the fat from the pan and place over high heat. Add the cognac, ignite it and reduce by about half. Pour in the duck stock and reduce this until only about 200ml/7floz remains.

To Serve

Return the duck breasts to the oven for about 1 minute to reheat.

Pour the sauce through a fine strainer or muslin on to the green peppercorns and keep warm. Melt the remaining butter in a pan. Gently warm the vegetables through in the butter and season them lightly. Divide the vegetables into neat piles in the centre of the plates. Spoon the sauce and peppercorns around these. Carve each duck breast into about 6 long slices and fan half on to the vegetables and half on to the sauce.

Goose

French: *Oie, Oison* German: *Gans* Italian: *Oca*

For a long time goose was considered the best of poultry and it found great favour in England, and was traditionally eaten at Michaelmas, in September. Its popularity now seems to have declined and goose seems difficult to find nowadays, probably because it is widely thought to be too greasy to eat or digest. This, I would say, is really the result of poor cooking rather than the fault of the goose. The greatest claim to fame for the goose however has to be its liver – foie gras – once described by a great French gourmet as 'the supreme fruit of gastronomy', which it undoubtedly must be.

Geese are at their best while still young, up to 6 months old, when they are known as 'goslings' or 'green geese'. From 6 months onwards they are then simply called geese. Beyond the age of 1 year the meat becomes very tough and is really only suitable for braising. Goslings are at their best between July and August, with geese at their best between September and January. When choosing a goose, look for fine grained pink flesh and a creamy white skin. If it still has its feet, then they should be soft, pliable and yellow, and its lower bill should, like all young birds, bend under the weight of the bird. As the goose ages, the feet and bill become much darker in colour.

Roast Goose

8 PORTIONS
1 goose, about 5kg/11lb
salt and freshly ground white
    pepper
175g/6oz mirepoix (leek,
    onion, celery, carrot)
600ml/1pt brown chicken stock
    (see page 198)
1 sprig of thyme
1 bay leaf
½ garlic clove
watercress and roast potatoes,
    to serve

Roast goose is traditionally served with apple sauce and sage and onion stuffing, the stuffing put into the goose before cooking. You could cook a stuffing separately, which would speed up the cooking of the goose a little. Save the fat that runs from the goose and use it whenever oil for frying is called for. Surrounded by watercress and served with roast potatoes, a good well-roasted goose is a fine meal indeed.

Method

Season the goose well on the inside with salt and pepper. Truss the bird (see pages 218–20). Using a sharp pointed knife, lightly score the skin in even lines on each breast and the legs. This will help the excess fat run from the goose during cooking. Season the outside of the goose and place it in a roasting pan. Pour about 5mm/¼ inch of water into the pan then place it into an oven heated to 240°C/475°F/gas 9. Roast for 45 minutes, basting occasionally. Turn the oven down to 200°C/400°F/gas 6 and roast for a further 1 hour, basting from time to time.

When the goose is cooked, remove it from the oven and place in a warm place to rest. Tip most of the fat from the roasting pan, add the vegetables and brown over high heat until golden. Pour in the chicken stock, add the herbs and garlic and simmer for 15 minutes, until reduced by about one-quarter.

To Serve

Return the goose to the oven for 10 minutes to reheat. Pour the sauce through a fine strainer or muslin into a sauceboat. Serve the goose with fresh, crisp watercress and roast potatoes.

Note

If the goose came with its neck, roughly chop and fry it along with the vegetables, allowing it to brown evenly.

MARINATED GOOSE BREASTS

This recipe was given to me by my good friend Sigurjon, who is the head chef of Naust restaurant in Reykjavik in Iceland. My wife and I had it as a first course at the restaurant last time we were over there and it was delicious. It is best using wild goose, but as it is illegal to sell wild geese in this country you must either shoot one yourself or know someone who has shot one and is willing to part with it. Alternatively, ordinary domestic goose will suffice.

8 PORTIONS
2 goose breasts
2 tsp rosemary leaves
2 tsp thyme leaves
25g/1oz parsley leaves
2 tsp coarse salt
10g/¼oz crushed black
  peppercorns
4 crushed juniper berries
1 tsp sugar
4 handfuls mixed salad leaves
  (corn salad, red oak leaf,
  curly endive, raddichio,
  lollo rosso, etc.)
salt and freshly ground white
  pepper
4 tbsp walnut oil
150g/5oz shelled walnuts
250ml/9floz tomato vinaigrette
  (see page 205)

Method

Remove all skin and fat from the goose breasts. Finely chop all the herbs and mix with the salt, crushed peppercorns, juniper berries and the sugar. Sprinkle about one-third of the mixture on to a plate or tray just large enough to take the goose breasts. Lay the two breasts on this then cover the breasts with the remaining mixture. Cover the tray with cling film to exclude the air. Leave this to marinate for 10 days in the refrigerator, turning the breasts in the marinade every day.

To Serve

Scrape the herbs etc. off the breasts and carve each breast into long, very thin slices. Wash and dry the salad leaves well. Lightly season them with salt and pepper and toss them in the walnut oil and walnuts. Place a neat pile of the salad leaves at 12 o'clock on each plate. Spoon the tomato vinaigrette on to the plates at 6 o'clock then lay the slices of goose half on the salad and half on the vinaigrette.

Confit of Goose

1 goose, weighing about
    5–5.5kg/11–12lb
1½ tbsp salt
50ml/2floz water
6 garlic cloves, peeled
1 tsp peppercorns
225g/8oz lard

This wonderful classical recipe is an excellent way of using goose, duck or even pork. Once sealed in its pot it will keep for up to 3 months. It was originally designed to be kept and eaten throughout the winter months. After this, I have also given a couple more recipes for using the confit once made.

Method

Remove the legs and breasts from the goose (see pages 216–17) and trim away all the excess fat and skin. Cut the legs into two to make drumsticks and thighs. Remove the thigh bone. Clean the end of the drumstick bone. Lay the pieces of goose on a tray and sprinkle the meat with the salt. Leave this in the refrigerator for 24 hours.

Remove all of the fat from the carcass and very finely dice or mince all of the fat and skin. Mix this with the water in a heavy-based pan. Place over very low heat and cook slowly for about 40 minutes until the fat has melted and is clear. Strain it through muslin or a fine strainer.

After 24 hours, brush the excess salt from the goose and place the pieces into the melted fat. Tie the garlic and peppercorns in muslin to make a bag and add to the fat. Cook over very low heat for 2½ hours.

Pour a little of the fat into the bottom of an earthenware pot, so that there is about 1cm/½ inch in the bottom and allow this to set. Once set, add the pieces of goose but do not allow them to touch the sides. Cover with the remaining fat and allow to set again. Melt the lard and pour over the top to form a seal.

SALAD OF CONFIT OF GOOSE WITH FOIE GRAS AND GIROLLES

Method

Remove the skin from the goose and slice the breast thinly into 4cm/1½ inch squares. Using a small knife, scrape away any dirt and root from the mushrooms. Pick through the lettuce leaves and wash and dry them well.

In a pan, heat 1 teaspoon of the goose fat, add the mushrooms, season and fry for about 30 seconds. Remove from the pan and pour off the fat. Add the vinegar and reduce it until almost gone. Add the Madeira and stock, bring to the boil and reduce slightly.

To Serve

Place the lettuce leaves into a bowl, lightly season, add the oil and mix in well. Arrange the leaves in neat piles in the centre of warmed plates. Return the mushrooms to the sauce and warm through over low heat. Heat a dry frying pan until very hot. Lightly season the foie gras and toss them into the pan. Quickly fry over high heat for about 15 seconds, turning occasionally. Drain and keep warm.

Drain the mushrooms from the sauce and place 5 on each plate around the lettuce. Pour the sauce on to the plates and arrange the slices of goose and foie gras around the lettuce. Put 3 tomatoes on to each plate, warm the remaining goose fat and spoon it over the meat. Finish the dish with chervil leaves scattered over.

4 PORTIONS

1 breast of confit goose (see page 48)
20 girolles
2 handfuls mixed lettuce leaves (curly endive, corn salad, raddichio, red oak leaf, lollo rosso)
1½ tbsp goose fat
salt and freshly ground white pepper
50ml/2floz sherry vinegar
50ml/2floz Madeira
120ml/4floz brown chicken stock (see page 198)
2 tbsp nut oil
150g/5oz foie gras, diced
12 cherry tomatoes
few fresh chervil leaves, to garnish

CONFIT OF GOOSE WITH PEAS

Method

Cut each goose breast into three and each thigh into two. Heat the goose fat in a heavy-based roasting pan and, when hot, add the goose and brown on the skin side. Remove from the pan and add the bacon and the shallots, browning these well. Remove the bacon and the shallots from the pan and pour off the fat. Pour in the white wine and reduce this over high heat until almost gone. Add the chicken stock and the pieces of goose, bring to the boil and cook in an oven heated to 220°C/425°F/gas 7. Add the shallots, bacon, shelled peas and sugar. Return to the oven and cook for about 10 minutes more or until the shallots and peas are cooked.

To Serve

Add the tarragon leaves and allow to infuse for a couple of minutes before serving. Remove the pieces of goose from the sauce. Spoon the sauce, vegetables and bacon on to the plates and divide the goose between them.

6 PORTIONS

1 confit goose (see page 48)
1½ tbsp goose fat
225g/8oz streaky bacon in one piece, diced
24 shallots, peeled
120ml/4floz dry white wine
450ml/¾pt brown chicken stock (see page 198)
350g/12oz shelled peas
1 tsp sugar
1 tbsp fresh tarragon leaves

GUINEA FOWL

French: *Pintade* German: *Perlhuhn* Italian: *Faraona*

Like the quail, the guinea fowl is not strictly poultry. Although it has never been a quarry species, it is really only semi-domesticated and would adapt quickly to living in the wild if allowed. The guinea fowl is a member of the pheasant family and originated in west Africa but has been reared in Europe since at least the fifteenth century. In fact, it is thought that when Shakespeare speaks of turkey he is actually referring to guinea fowl. Although the flesh of the wild guinea fowl is said to be inedible, the flesh of the domestic guinea fowl tastes like a cross between chicken and pheasant with a slightly gamey flavour, and a texture more like that of pheasant. The plumage of the guinea fowl is quite unusual, with each dark grey feather spotted white, giving a blue metallic appearance when seen in the sunlight. The average saleable weight of a guinea fowl would be 1–1.2kg/2¼–2½lb dressed weight, but it has a much heavier bone structure than a chicken and less meat content, so a bird of this size is only sufficient for two people. The best age for guinea fowl is between 8 and 9 weeks. Any older and the meat toughens quite considerably as well as becoming very dry. Any recipe for chicken or pheasant would also suit guinea fowl.

Sautéed and Braised Guinea Fowl with Two Sauces

Whenever I serve this dish I always serve a small open apple tart on the plate with it, both as a garnish to the dish and for the contrast in flavours and texture.

Method

Remove the legs and breasts from the guinea fowls (see pages 216–17). Draw the sinews from the legs. Trim the breasts of excess skin and fat and remove the sinew from the fillets. Bone the legs, roll them and tie in shape with string. Roughly chop the bones from one of the birds.

Heat half of the oil in a roasting pan and add half of the butter. Lightly season the rolled legs and sear in the hot fat, browning slightly. Remove from the pan. Add the bones and brown these well. Remove from the pan and add the vegetables, cooking until brown. Pour off the fat, add the white wine and reduce by half. Add 325ml/11floz of the stock. Bring to the boil, and return the legs and the bones to this along with the herbs and garlic. Braise in an oven heated to 220°C/425°F/gas 7 for 25 minutes.

While the legs are cooking, heat the remaining oil in a frying pan. Lightly season the breasts, add the remaining butter and, when sizzling, add the breasts, skin side down. Sauté for about 5 minutes each side. When cooked remove the breasts and keep warm. Pour off the fat from the pan, add the Calvados and reduce by half. Add the remaining stock and reduce by half. Pour in the cream, bring to the boil then strain the sauce through a fine strainer and keep it warm. When the legs are cooked, remove them from the sauce and keep them in a warm place. Strain the sauce through muslin and reduce it until only 175ml/6floz remains.

To Serve

Remove the strings from the legs. Cut each leg into 6 slices at a slight angle. Return these along with the breasts to the oven for a couple of minutes to reheat. Pour the cream sauce on to one half of each plate, then pour two-thirds of the braising sauce on to the other half. Place a breast on to the cream sauce and a sliced leg on to the dark sauce. Spoon the remaining dark sauce over the legs. Finish with a sprig of fresh dill and the warmed apple tarts, if using them.

4 PORTIONS
2 guinea fowls
1½ tbsp oil
25g/1oz unsalted butter
salt and freshly ground white pepper
1 stalk celery, roughly chopped
2 shallots, roughly chopped
85ml/3floz dry white wine
450ml/¾pt brown chicken stock (see page 198)
1 sprig of rosemary
1 sprig of thyme
1 garlic clove, roughly chopped
85ml/3floz Calvados
120ml/4floz double cream
4 sprigs of dill

BREAST OF GUINEA FOWL WITH YELLOW PEPPERS

4 PORTIONS

4 guinea fowl breasts

salt and freshly ground white
    pepper

1 tsp oil

100g/3½oz unsalted butter

175ml/6floz dry white wine

2 shallots, finely diced

300ml/10floz veal stock (see
    page 201)

⅓ tsp finely crushed black
    peppercorns

juice of ¼ lemon

120ml/4floz chicken stock (see
    page 198)

50ml/2floz double cream

2 yellow peppers, skinned,
    deseeded and cut into a
    julienne

Method

Remove any excess skin and fat from the guinea fowl breasts and remove the sinew from the fillet. Lightly season the breasts. Heat the oil and 15g/½oz of the butter in a frying pan. When it is sizzling, lay the breasts in skin side down and fry gently for 5 minutes, browning lightly. Turn the breasts over and continue frying for a further 5 minutes. Once cooked, remove them from the pan and keep warm. Tip the fat from the pan and pour in 120ml/4floz of the white wine, add the shallots and reduce until the wine has almost evaporated. Pour in the veal stock and reduce until only about 200ml/7floz remains.

Place the remaining wine, the crushed peppercorns, the lemon juice and the chicken stock in a separate saucepan and reduce until almost gone. Add the cream and the yellow peppers, return to the boil then gradually add the remaining butter, shaking the pan continuously until it has all melted. Season to taste then keep warm.

To Serve

Add any juice that runs from the breasts to the sauce. Place the guinea fowl in an oven heated to 230°C/450°F/gas 8 for 2 minutes to reheat. Strain the sauce through a fine strainer or muslin. Divide the sauce evenly on to the centre of the plates. Cut each breast into two horizontally, starting at the point of the breast but stopping just before the wing bone. Fan each breast on to the sauce on the plates, then spoon the yellow peppers over the breasts.

BREAST OF GUINEA FOWL WITH TOMATOES AND SPRING ONIONS

Method

Remove any excess skin and fat from the guinea fowl breasts and remove the sinew from each fillet.

Blanch the tomatoes, then skin and deseed, saving the skins and seeds for the sauce. Cut the flesh into small neat dice. Trim the spring onions of their roots and pull off any outer leaves. Cut off the white parts to about 4cm/1.5 inches and discard the green tops. Blanch the onions in boiling salted water for 15 seconds, refresh and drain.

Lightly season the breasts. Heat the oil and 15g/½oz of the butter in a frying pan. When it is sizzling, place in the breasts skin side down and fry gently for 5 minutes, browning lightly. Turn the breasts over and continue frying for a further 5 minutes. Once cooked, remove the breasts from the pan and keep warm. Tip off the fat, add 15g/½oz of the butter and quickly fry the onions, browning them lightly. Remove from the pan and keep warm with the breasts. Add the chopped shallots and the garlic and lightly fry for about 30 seconds. Pour in the white wine and add the tomato skins and seeds. Reduce until the wine has almost evaporated. Pour in the stock and reduce until only about 200ml/7floz remains.

To Serve

Add any juices that have run from the breasts during resting to the sauce, then place the breasts and the onions in an oven heated to 230°C/450°F/gas 8 for 2 minutes to reheat. Strain the sauce through a fine strainer or muslin on to the diced tomato and tarragon leaves. Return the sauce to the boil, remove it from the heat and gradually add the remaining butter to the sauce, shaking the pan continuously until all the butter has melted. Cut each breast into 5 or 6 thick slices across and at a slight angle. Spoon a little of the sauce on to the centre of each plate and arrange a sliced breast on top. Place 5 spring onions evenly around the sliced breasts and spoon the remaining sauce over and around the guinea fowl.

4 PORTIONS

4 guinea fowl breasts
5 tomatoes
20 spring onions
salt and freshly ground white pepper
2 tsp oil
50g/2oz unsalted butter
2 shallots, finely diced
½ garlic clove, crushed
120ml/4floz dry white wine
300ml/10floz brown chicken stock (see page 198)
½ tsp tarragon leaves, chopped

Roasted Guinea Fowl with
Shallots and Garlic
(see page 56)

ROASTED GUINEA FOWL WITH SHALLOTS AND GARLIC

2 PORTIONS

1 guinea fowl
2 tsp oil
15g/½oz unsalted butter
salt and freshly ground white
    pepper
6 garlic cloves, peeled
6 shallots, peeled
50ml/2floz dry white wine
225ml/8floz brown chicken
    stock (see page 198)
1 sprig of rosemary

Method

Truss the guinea fowl (see pages 218–20). Heat half the oil in a roasting pan and when hot add the butter. Sear the guinea fowl, browning slightly on all sides. Place it on its back and season. Cook in an oven heated to 220°C/425°F/gas 7 for 20 minutes, basting occasionally. After 15 minutes add the garlic and shallots to the pan. Turn them in the fat and season lightly.

Once cooked, remove the guinea fowl, garlic and shallots from the pan and allow the bird to rest for 10 minutes. Then remove the trussing string from the guinea fowl and cut away the legs and the breasts. Cut each leg in two – into the thigh and drumstick. Trim the ends of the drumsticks and remove the thigh bone. Cover the meat and leave, with the shallots and garlic, in a warm place.

Roughly chop the bones. Pour off the fat from the roasting pan and add the remaining oil. Brown the bones well. Pour off the oil, add the white wine and reduce by half. Add the chicken stock and the rosemary and simmer for about 10 minutes. Strain the sauce through a very fine strainer or muslin.

To Serve

Return the guinea fowl, shallots and garlic to the oven for about 2 minutes to reheat.

Arrange 3 shallots and 3 garlic cloves around the plates. Place a boned thigh in the centre of each plate, half cover this with a breast and then top with a drumstick. Pour the sauce over and around.

Breast of Guinea Fowl with a Mousse of Its Livers

Method

Trim the livers of any sinew and gall bladder stain. Place these along with the garlic and a little salt and pepper into a food processor and process until smooth. Add the egg, pour in the port, then gradually add 150ml/¼pt of the cream. Pass this mixture through a fine strainer, then test the mousse by dropping a teaspoon of the mixture into boiling water, if it is too firm, add a little more cream and test again. Leave in the refrigerator until needed.

Trim the baby leeks of their outer leaves and cut off their leafy tops. Blanch the leeks in boiling salted water for a few seconds then refresh in iced water. Once cold, cut into 5cm/2 inch pieces.

Lightly butter 4 individual oval or round moulds and pour in the liver mixture. Cover each one with a little lightly buttered foil and place these into a roasting pan half-filled with boiling water. Cook in an oven heated to 200°C/400°F/gas 6 for 12–15 minutes. Keep warm. Lightly season the breasts. Heat the oil in a frying pan and, when hot, add 15g/½oz of the butter. Lay the breasts in, skin side down, and gently fry for about 5 minutes, turn them over and cook for a further 5 minutes. Keep warm. Pour off the fat from the pan. Over a high heat add the white wine and reduce until it has almost gone. Pour in the stock and reduce this by almost half.

To Serve

Reheat the mousses along with the breasts in the oven for about 2 minutes.

Using a little of the butter, gently reheat the leeks rolling them in the warm butter until hot. Place a neat pile of the leeks towards one edge of the plates. Carefully tip out the mousses and place them a couple of inches away from the leeks. Carve each guinea fowl breast into about 5 slices and fan them on to the plates opposite the mousses. Add the remaining cream to the sauce and return it to the boil. Over a low heat, gradually whisk in the remaining butter, piece by piece, until all the butter has melted. Pour the sauce through a fine strainer or muslin and pour it into the middle of the plates.

4 PORTIONS

4 guinea fowl breasts, trimmed of excess fat and sinew
85g/3oz guinea fowl livers
½ garlic glove
salt and freshly ground white pepper
1 egg
40ml/1½floz port
175ml/6floz double cream
4 pencil-thin baby leeks
115g/4oz cold unsalted butter, diced, plus extra for greasing
2 tsp oil
85ml/3floz dry white wine
200ml/7floz brown chicken stock (see page 198)

Breast of Guinea Fowl with Lentils

BREAST OF GUINEA FOWL WITH WILD MUSHROOMS AND A TRUFFLE SAUCE

This recipe will work equally well with pheasant or chicken. If a mixture of mushrooms is not available then only use one type.

Method

Lightly season the breasts. Using a small knife, carefully scrape away any dirt from the mushrooms. Heat the oil in a frying pan, add half of the butter and when sizzling add the breasts, skin side down. Fry gently for 5 minutes on each side. Remove and keep warm.

Pour off the fat from the pan and add the remaining butter. Quickly fry the mushrooms for 2 minutes over high heat, seasoning them lightly. Remove from the pan and keep warm. Pour off the fat. Add the Madeira and reduce by half over high heat. Add the stock and the truffle juice and reduce by half again.

To Serve

Place the guinea fowl breasts and the wild mushrooms in an oven heated to 220°C/425°F/gas 7 for 2 minutes to reheat.

Strain the sauce through a fine strainer or muslin on to the diced truffle. Divide the mushrooms into equal piles in the centre of the plates. Cut each breast into 5 thick slices across, fan these half on the mushrooms and half on the plates, and pour the sauce around.

4 PORTIONS
4 guinea fowl breasts, trimmed of excess fat
200g/7oz mixed wild mushrooms (girolles, pleurots, shiitakes, morels)
2 tsp oil
25g/1oz unsalted butter
salt and freshly ground white pepper
85ml/3floz Madeira
300ml/½pt brown chicken stock (see page 198)
50ml/2floz truffle juice
15g/½oz truffle, diced (optional)

BREAST OF GUINEA FOWL WITH LENTILS

Method

Lightly season the guinea fowl breasts. Heat the oil in a saucepan, add the butter and fry the breasts, skin side down first, for about 5 minutes on each side until lightly browned. Remove from the pan and leave in a warm place.

Pour off the fat from the pan. Quickly fry the bacon in the pan until golden brown. Add the white wine and reduce over high heat until it has almost gone. Add the chicken stock and bring to the boil. Add the lentils to the boiling stock. Simmer for 15 minutes. Add the thyme leaves for the last 2 minutes.

To Serve

Place the guinea fowl breasts in an oven heated to 220°C/425°F/gas 7 for about 2 minutes to reheat.

Add the diced tomato to the sauce and spoon on to the plates. Cut each breast in half lengthways, but leave joined at one end. Fan each breast, place in the centre of the plate and top each breast with a sprig of thyme.

4 PORTIONS
4 guinea fowl breasts, trimmed of excess fat, with wing bone
salt and freshly ground white pepper
2 tsp oil
15g/½oz unsalted butter
50g/2oz bacon, diced
120ml/4floz dry white wine
350ml/12floz chicken stock (see page 198)
50g/2oz lentils, rinsed twice in cold water
1 tsp fresh thyme leaves
1 tomato, blanched, skinned, seeded and diced
4 sprigs of fresh thyme

Braised Guinea Fowl with Cabbage

4 PORTIONS

1 guinea fowl

salt and freshly ground white
pepper

2 tsp oil

1 bacon bone

1 stalk celery, roughly
chopped

½ small onion, roughly
chopped

85ml/3floz dry white wine

300ml/½pt brown chicken
stock (see page 198)

1 garlic clove, roughly
chopped

1 bay leaf

1 sprig of fresh thyme

85g/3oz bacon

175g/6oz savoy cabbage

15g/½oz unsalted butter

Method

Remove the legs and breasts from the guinea fowl (see pages 216–17). Trim the breasts of any excess skin, fat and sinew. Remove the knuckle from the leg and lightly season the flesh. Finely chop all the bones. Heat the oil in a frying pan and quickly sear the legs and breasts until lightly browned. Remove from the pan then add the chopped bones along with the bacon bone. Fry these until they are evenly browned, add the chopped vegetables and continue frying until the vegetables have browned.

Transfer the bones and vegetables to an ovenproof dish. Lay the breasts and legs on top of these. Deglaze the frying pan with the white wine and reduce by half. Add the chicken stock and bring to the boil. Pour this on to the guinea fowl and add the garlic and herbs. Cover the pan and place in an oven heated to 200°C/400°F/gas 6. After 25 minutes remove the breasts and return the legs to the oven for a further 25 minutes.

Remove the legs from the pan, strain the sauce through a fine strainer and reduce it by half. Cut the bacon into lardons. Remove any outer leaves and the core from the cabbage. Finely shred the remaining leaves and wash well. Fry the bacon lardons in a saucepan until they are nicely browned. Add the butter and, when it is sizzling, add the cabbage, stir well and cover the pan with a tight fitting lid. Cook the cabbage for 3–4 minutes, stirring occasionally.

To Serve

Return the breasts and the legs to the sauce for a few minutes to reheat. Once the cabbage is cooked, drain it from the pan. Place a pile of cabbage in the centre of each plate. Place 1 leg and 1 breast on the top of each pile. Strain the sauce again through a fine strainer or muslin and pour around the cabbage.

TURKEY

French: *Dinde* German: *Pute* Italian: *Tacchino*

The turkey tends to be thought about in Britain only at Christmas time. After Christmas day, everyone has had enough. It is in fact a much more versatile bird than you may first imagine – there is more to it than plainly roasted with chestnut stuffing. Surprisingly, it was not until about the eighteenth century that turkey first appeared in this country – and even later than that before it was associated with Christmas. It was brought over from its native America, where it is still to be found in the wild, although in decreasing numbers.

Guinea fowl, when first introduced to this country, was called 'turkey' and when the turkey as we now know it was introduced, it was thought to be a larger variety of the same species, probably due to the similar plumage and head. Turkey ranges in weight from about 2.75kg/6lb through to 14kg/30lb plus, the best ones being in the smaller to mid-weight range. Although I do think turkey is versatile, I have only given two recipes for it. This is basically because it's not a bird I often have occasion to use. Use it in any chicken recipe, but remember its flesh is much drier and coarser than chicken and will need more care during cooking.

Escalopes of Turkey with Tomato and Thyme

4 PORTIONS

8 turkey escalopes, weighing
about 85g/3oz each

salt and freshly ground white
pepper

2 tsp oil

100g/3½oz cold unsalted
butter, diced

50ml/2floz dry white wine

225ml/8floz chicken stock (see
page 198)

juice of ¼ lemon

½ tsp Dijon mustard

1 shallot, finely chopped

1½ tbsp fresh thyme leaves

2 tomatoes, blanched, peeled,
seeded and diced

85ml/3floz whipped double
cream

4 sprigs of fresh thyme

This is a very simple but effective dish which takes very little preparation or cooking. A few years ago it would have been very difficult to find turkey escalopes, nowadays every supermarket stocks them. If you have no fresh thyme, any other herb will do; try basil, chives or even mint.

Method

Lightly season the turkey escalopes. Heat the oil in a frying pan. Add 15g/½oz of the butter and, when it is sizzling, fry the escalopes for about 1½ minutes on each side. Remove them from the pan and keep warm. Pour off the fat, add the white wine and reduce over high heat until almost gone. Pour in the chicken stock and lemon juice and add the mustard. Bring to the boil and reduce until only 85ml/3floz remains.

To Serve

Place the escalopes in an oven heated to 220°C/425°F/gas 7 for about 2 minutes to reheat.

Add the chopped shallot and the thyme to the reduced stock. Place the pan over low heat and gradually whisk in the remaining butter, piece by piece, until it has melted. Add the diced tomato and stir in the whipped cream. Spoon two-thirds of the sauce on to serving plates. Lay two escalopes on each plate and spoon the remaining sauce over these. Finish each plate with a sprig of fresh thyme to garnish.

Escalopes of Turkey with Tomato and Thyme

Roulade of Turkey with Morels

6 PORTIONS

6 turkey escalopes, each
    weighing 125–150g/4½–5oz
25g/1oz dried morels
85g/3oz fresh turkey
½ tsp salt
1 egg white
150ml/¼pt double cream
2 tsp Madeira
salt and freshly ground white
    pepper
600ml/1pt brown chicken stock
    (see page 198)
120ml/4floz dry white wine
40g/1½oz unsalted butter
1 shallot, finely chopped
150g/5oz rice
300ml/½pt chicken stock (see
    page 198)
1 bay leaf
2 pinches of saffron powder

Method

Soak the dried morels in cold water for at least 12 hours before they are needed. Roughly chop the 85g/3oz of turkey and place it in a food processor with the salt and process until smooth. Add the egg white and process until it starts to stiffen. Rub this mixture through a fine strainer into a bowl set over ice. Gradually add the cream, mixing it in well each time. Stir in the Madeira. Drain the morels from the water then rinse well in clean water. Drain them again then squeeze them dry. Mix into the turkey mousse mixture. Test the mousse for consistency and seasoning by dropping a teaspoon of the mixture into boiling water. If the mousse is too firm then add a little more cream and test again.

Using a cutlet bat or the side of a heavy-bladed knife, flatten each of the turkey escalopes between two sheets of cling film. Lightly season each escalope, then divide the mousse between them and roll each one into a fat sausage shape. Roll each one in a strip of greaseproof paper – this will keep their shape.

Place the turkey rolls in a roasting pan, and pour in the brown chicken stock and the white wine. Cover the pan and bring it to the boil. Just as it starts to simmer, transfer it to an oven heated to 220°C/425°F/gas 7. Cook for 12 minutes. Melt 15g/½oz of the butter, add the shallot and fry gently, without colouring, until it starts to soften. Add the rice and turn it through the butter until well coated. Pour in the chicken stock, add the bay leaf and a little seasoning. Cover with a sheet of buttered greaseproof paper. Bring to the boil then transfer it to the oven and cook for 8 minutes. When the rice is cooked, remove the paper, discard the bay leaf and dot the rice with 15g/½oz of the butter, replace the paper and keep the rice warm. When the turkey rolls are cooked, carefully remove them from the stock, pour a little of the stock over them to prevent them drying out, cover and keep in a warm place.

To Serve

Add the saffron to the stock and reduce this until only about 350ml/ 12floz remains. Stir some of the butter through the rice then press it into 6 individual dariole moulds. Return these along with the turkey to the oven for 2 minutes to reheat. Tip a timbale of rice on to the centre of each plate. Remove the paper from the turkey rolls and carve each roll into 5 thick slices, discarding the ends. Gradually add the remaining butter to the sauce, piece by piece, until it has all melted. Pour the sauce around the rice. Place 5 slices of turkey around this.

FEATHERED GAME

*The game bird is probably the type of game you think of first,
and the one most widely used. This is possibly due to the fact
that there are many more types of feathered game than furred,
especially in Britain. Pheasants are shot in their millions each
year and that number still seems to rise. Gone are the days
when the medium-sized shoot could easily sell all of their
surplus birds. As more and more EEC agricultural grants
become available to the farmer to put his land to other uses, the
more they are turning to shooting, and pheasant and partridge
rearing, as an alternative or extra income. This is, of course,
good news for the consumer. Always thought of as an expensive
meat, game is now becoming cheaper. Not that I have ever
considered it expensive. Pound for pound it is better value for
money than most other meats. Of course, there is much more to
feathered game than pheasant and partridge, but here I have
concentrated only on the birds most commonly available in
Europe. Although ptarmigan and capercaillie, for instance,
are shot and eaten, it is very unlikely that either would be
found for sale very often. Wild ducks are widely shot in this
country but I have only given recipes for two types, mallard
and teal, as these are the most common. Widgeon and pintail
are not shot in sufficient numbers and will rarely be seen for
sale. Of all the game birds, however, my personal preference
would be the distinguished woodcock. Not only does it excite
my palette but presents an exciting challenge to the hunter.
Wood pigeon is a very underrated source of food in this
country, and I wonder if, because it is classed as vermin rather
than game, people are put off by the idea.*

A lot of the pleasure in eating game comes from the hunt that preceeds it to the pot – and the best of the bag is always taken by the hunter. When choosing your game great care is needed. If you have shot the bird yourself or been given it by a friend then freshness is not a problem. If you are buying the bird from a game dealer, butcher or supermarket, apart from obviously looking fresh, it should not have an unpleasant odour, and the skin, if the bird is plucked, should be dry, not moist. If it is still in the feather, then the eyes should be bright not sunken and dull. The feathers should also still have a lustre and not be dull and lifeless. If your game dealer knows his trade, he will also be able to tell you when, and often where, it was shot.

The hanging of game is a subject open to debate. Some people say that game is not fit to eat until it is 'high' but my personal opinion is that it is best eaten fairly fresh, with the exception of pheasant. All game should be hung before plucking, by the neck, in a cold airy place with plenty of space around each bird to allow the air to circulate freely. Pheasant needs to be hung before plucking for 8–10 days, but it can be kept longer if the weather is particularly cold. Grouse on the other hand, being such a strongly flavoured bird anyway, should not be hung for more than 3 days. For the rest of the game birds I find 5–7 days about right under cold conditions and an extra 2 days during really cold weather.

The age of the bird is also of paramount importance. A bird of up to one year old will make very good eating, after that, especially with grouse, it starts to become dry and tough. The general rule of thumb for young birds is that if you hold the bird by its bottom beak it will not hold its own weight without bending. Of course, if the bird has already been prepared than there really is no sure way of knowing until you start to eat it.

GROUSE

French: *Grouse, Gelinotte, Coq de Bruyère*. German: *Auerhahn*

'The glorious twelfth' – the first day of the grouse season. All the publicity and media hysteria it brings with it is probably the only thing the majority of people know of the grouse, that is, except of course that one always associates it with Scotland. This is not the only place it is to be found – Yorkshire, Durham, and Lancashire are also good grouse areas. For many years the grouse was claimed as Britain's own native game bird, exclusive to the British Isles, to be found nowhere else in the world. It was in fact granted full species status by the British Ornithologists Union in 1952. It is now accepted that the grouse is actually only a sub-species of the willow grouse of which there are 15 other sub-species, and they are to be found throughout the northern hemisphere in North America, Europe and Asia. However, we are not entirely wrong to claim it as being unique to Britain because it is the only sub-species that does not turn white during the winter months.

Although most people would recognize a grouse when hanging in a game dealer's window, it is quite difficult to describe accurately. The colouring and patterns of the plumage vary with the season and locality, but basically the male grouse is a deep brown and its body feathers are finely grained with spots and thin lines. The hen is more of a tawny brown and its body feathers bear heavy bars. All grouse have feathered legs and toes – no other bird has this. The difference between male and female is, however, not as important as the difference between young and old. This difference is essential, because if faced with a grouse for the first time, and it happens to be old, whether you are cooking it or just eating it, it will be enough to put you off grouse for life.

In the first few weeks of the season, the young grouse can be judged purely on size but they mature quickly and, once September comes, this is no longer a good guideline. The four main ways of telling young from old are: the lower beak will not hold the weight of the bird without breaking; if using only your thumb the skull can easily be crushed; the third primary feather is shorter than the others; and the first two primary feathers in a young bird are pointed – in an old bird they will be rounded.

It is true to say that the meat of the grouse has a powerful flavour, by far the strongest of all our game birds, and it will not suit everyone. Personally, I do not like grouse that has been hung for more than 3 days because, as it ages, its gamey flavour increases considerably. Although it is in season from the 12th of August until the 10th of December, I find the early birds to be the best, that is, from August to at the latest the middle of October.

ROAST GROUSE

The traditional way of serving grouse is with fried breadcrumbs, rowan or redcurrant jelly, bread sauce, game chips and watercress. There really is no need to serve all of these garnishes – the more essential items are the jelly, bread sauce and watercress. Some people say that if you need to serve a gravy with it then it has been overcooked. Personally, I do like a little sauce to go with it.

4 PORTIONS
4 young grouse
salt and freshly ground white
  pepper
4 slices of streaky bacon
1 tbsp oil
25g/1oz unsalted butter
½ small onion
1 stalk celery
1 small carrot
85ml/3floz red wine
300ml/½pt brown chicken
  stock (see page 198)
watercress, to garnish
rowan or redcurrant jelly
bread sauce (see page 202)

Method

Truss the grouse (see pages 218–20). Season them lightly and tie the bacon loosely over the breasts. Heat the oil and half the butter in a roasting pan and quickly seal the grouse on all sides. Place the grouse on to one leg and roast in an oven heated to 230°C/450°F/gas 8 for 5 minutes. Turn the grouse over on to the other leg and return to the oven for a further 5 minutes. Turn the birds on to their backs and continue cooking for 5 more minutes. Rest in a warm place for about 10 minutes. Peel the vegetables and roughly chop.

When the birds have rested, remove the legs and breasts and keep warm. Roughly chop the carcasses. Pour off the fat from the roasting pan and add the remaining butter. Add the chopped carcasses and the vegetables to this and brown them well. Pour off the fat and place over high heat. Add the red wine and reduce by half. Pour in the chicken stock and simmer gently for 10 minutes.

To Serve

Return the grouse to the oven for 2 minutes to reheat.

Pour the sauce through a fine strainer or muslin. Arrange the grouse on the plates, legs first, side by side, then the breast on top. Pour some sauce over and around the birds and serve the remaining sauce in a sauceboat. Garnish with a sprig of watercress, and serve rowan or redcurrant jelly and the bread sauce separately.

ROAST GROUSE WITH ORANGES AND BLACKBERRIES

Method

Truss the grouse (see pages 218–20). Peel and segment the oranges. Remove the pith from the peel and cut half of the peel into fine julienne. Roughly chop the remaining peel. Bring the sugar and water to the boil, throw in the julienne and cook until only about 2 teaspoons of the liquid remains. Leave to go cold. Save the 20 best blackberries to use as garnish later and purée the remainder. Rub the purée through a sieve to remove the seeds.

Season the grouse. Heat the oil in a roasting pan and, when hot, add half the butter. Quickly sear the grouse in the hot fat on all sides. Place the grouse on to one leg and roast in an oven heated to 230°C/450°F/gas 8 for 5 minutes. Turn the grouse over on to the other leg and roast for a further 5 minutes. Turn the birds on to their backs and cook for a final 5 minutes. Remove them from the pan and allow to rest in a warm place for about 10 minutes.

Remove the legs and breasts from the birds and keep warm. Roughly chop the carcasses. Pour off the fat from the pan and add the remaining butter. Brown the chopped carcasses in this. Pour off the fat, place the pan over high heat, add the vinegar and reduce this until gone. Pour in the red wine and reduce by half. Pour in the stock and add the blackberry purée, the roughly chopped orange peel and any juice both from the oranges and the grouse. Bring this to the boil and allow to simmer for 15 minutes. Pour the sauce through a fine strainer or muslin. If the sauce is a little too sharp then add a little of the syrup from the julienne. Keep warm.

To Serve

Reheat the grouse in the oven for a couple of minutes.

Arrange the saved blackberries in neat piles at the top of each plate. Arrange the orange segments either side of these. Place 2 legs in the centre of each plate and top with 2 breasts. Pour the sauce over and around the grouse. Drain the julienne from the syrup and place a neat pile on the centre of each grouse.

4 PORTIONS

4 young grouse
2 oranges
2 tsp sugar
120ml/4floz water
150g/5oz blackberries
salt and freshly ground white
    pepper
1½ tbsp oil
25g/1oz unsalted butter
50ml/2floz red wine vinegar
85ml/3floz red wine
225ml/8floz game stock (see
    page 200)

*Roast Grouse with Oranges and
Blackberries (see page 69)*

TERRINE OF GROUSE

Grouse terrine marries very well with quince jelly – the strong pungent flavour of the grouse is well complemented by the delicate sweetness of the rose pink jelly (see page 204). Try melting it down, adding a touch of white wine and a little gelatine, then setting it on the plates like a pink mirror. Serve a little mixed autumn leaf salad on a side dish, accompanied by slices of warm homemade walnut bread.

MAKES ABOUT 20 PORTIONS
4 young grouse
2 tsp oil
120ml/4floz veal stock (see page 201)
115g/4oz mirepoix (leek, celery, carrot and shallot)
50ml/2floz red wine
1 garlic clove
1 sprig of fresh thyme
175g/6oz piece of smoked bacon
175g/6oz piece of pork fat
salt and freshly ground white pepper
25ml/1floz Madeira
25ml/1floz port
1 orange
225g/8oz chicken livers
3 eggs
275g/10oz fresh girolles
8–10 thin slices of pork back fat

Method

Save the grouse livers. Remove the legs and breasts (see pages 216–17) and cut the meat from the leg bones. Roughly chop the bones and carcasses. Brown them in the oil in a roasting pan in an oven heated to 240°C/475°F/gas 9. Once nicely browned, transfer them to a saucepan, add the stock and cover with water. Bring to the boil, skimming as necessary. Lightly brown the mirepoix in the roasting pan, then transfer to the stock. Pour off the fat from the pan and deglaze with the red wine. Add this to the stock along with the garlic and thyme. Simmer the stock for 1 hour. Pour through a fine strainer and reduce over high heat until only about 40ml/1½floz remains. Leave to cool.

Cut the breasts, leg meat, bacon and pork fat into 6mm/¼ inch dice. Place in a bowl, season and pour over the Madeira and port. Grate the zest and squeeze the juice from the orange and add to the meat. Mix well and leave to stand for 3–4 hours.

Remove any sinews, fat and gall bladder stain from the grouse and chicken livers. Roughly chop or mince them, season and mix in the eggs. Cut away any root and brush off any dirt from the girolles then cut them into 1cm/½ inch dice. Mix the livers and girolles with the diced meat.

Line a 28cm/11 inch terrine with the thin slices of fat, overlapping them slightly and leaving an overhang long enough to wrap over the top of the terrine. Stir the cold stock into the meat mixture. It is essential that the meat is distributed evenly. Fill the terrine and fold over the overhanging fat to totally enclose the filling. Cover with a sheet of foil and cover with the lid.

Place the terrine in a roasting pan half-filled with boiling water. Cook in an oven heated to 140°C/275°F/gas 1 for 1½ hours. Test the mousse to see whether or not it is cooked by pushing a skewer into the centre – it should come out warm not hot. Leave the terrine to cool. Place a weight on top and leave to go cold. Transfer the terrine to the refrigerator to chill for at least 24 hours.

PARTRIDGE

French: *Perdreau* German: *Rebhuhn* Italian: *Pernice*

The partridge, more especially the grey or English partridge, has probably been field sports' greatest victim of modern farming. During the 1800s, the grey partridge would have been our most common of game birds, now, thanks to what has been described as 'prairie farming' and the use of chemical sprays, they are hard to find. The red-legged partridge, or French partridge as it is also known, is to be found much more readily ever since its introduction to this country from France in the seventeenth century. It is a much easier bird to rear than the English and easier to hold in a given area. However, it is not as highly prized or sought after as our own native bird. Both the grey and red partridges are to be found throughout Europe and into Russia, with other species in Asia and North America.

They really are two very distinctly different birds, the grey being quite small and relatively drab looking in appearance – that is until closer inspection. As with the wood pigeon, the beauty of the grey partridge's splendid plumage is not revealed until close up. The small neat rounded body has mainly dull brown upper feathers with chestnut bars. Underneath, the feathers are mainly grey with pale orange across the neck and face. The wings are splashed with cream, and both sexes have a brown horseshoe marking on the chest which is more prominent in the male. Comparatively, the red-legged partridge is quite splendid and considerably larger. It has a striking white bib topped with a bright red bill and a black stripe over its eyes, and, of course, its red legs from which it undoubtedly derives its name.

On their culinary attributes, the English partridge comes out tops. It is a far superior bird being smaller with a finer flavour and texture. The meat is also a much paler colour. Both English and French partridge are in season from the 1st of September to the 1st of February but early birds, up to November, are best. Young birds are detectable by their flexible beaks and pointed, rather than rounded, flight feathers.

Roast Partridge with Cèpes

Roast Partridge with Cèpes

Happily, the partridge season begins just at the time when cèpes are at their best and most prolific. As in many cases, the best accompaniment for a dish is an ingredient that is in season at the same time. This is certainly true of the cèpe and the partridge. The partridge is at its best while still young, and the cèpe, probably the best of all edible fungi, can be found in deciduous woods everywhere during September.

Method

Remove the wish bones from the partridges and truss the birds (see pages 218–20). Lightly season the birds inside and out and cut each slice of bacon in two, wrap around the birds and tie with string. Using a small sharp knife, trim off any root and brush off any dirt from the cèpes but do not wash them. Remove the caps and set to one side, and cut the stalks into small dice.

Heat the oil in a roasting pan then add 15g/½oz of the butter. Sear the birds in the hot fat on all sides. Place them on one leg and cook in an oven heated to 230°C/450°F/gas 8 for 4 minutes. Turn the birds on to the other leg and roast for a further 4 minutes. Leave to rest for about 10 minutes then remove the legs and the breasts from all of the birds and keep warm.

Cut the bacon into dice. Roughly chop the carcasses. Melt the remaining butter in the roasting pan and lightly brown the bones. Pour off the fat, add the white wine and reduce over a high heat until almost gone. Pour in the Madeira and reduce by half. Add the stocks and simmer until about 175ml/6floz remains.

To Serve

Return the partridges to the oven for a couple of minutes to reheat. Melt the remaining butter and brush the caps of the cèpes, lightly season, then grill on both sides under a hot grill for about 3 minutes.

Pour the sauce through a fine strainer into a clean pan and return it to the boil. Add the diced cèpes and bacon and simmer for 1 minute. Place a grilled cap in the centre of each plate, place 2 legs on top of it, then sit 2 breasts over the legs. Pour the sauce both over the partridge and on to the plates.

4 PORTIONS

4 young partridges
salt and freshly ground white
    pepper
4 slices of streaky bacon, rinds
    removed
350g/12oz fresh cèpes
2 tsp oil
20g/¾oz unsalted butter
50ml/2floz dry white wine
120ml/4floz Madeira
225ml/8floz brown chicken or
    pheasant stock (see page 198
    or 200)
85ml/3floz veal stock (see page
    201)

Braised Partridge on a Bed of Lentils

4 portions
4 partridges
115g/4oz brown lentils
50g/2oz unsalted butter
2 shallots, finely diced
50g/2oz streaky bacon, diced
300ml/½pt chicken stock (see
    page 198)
salt and freshly ground white
    pepper
1 bay leaf
2 tsp oil
115g/4oz mirepoix (celery,
    onion, carrot)
85ml/3floz red wine
300ml/½pt brown chicken
    stock (see page 198)
1 sprig of fresh thyme
1 garlic clove, roughly
    chopped

Method

Truss the partridges (see pages 218–20). Carefully pick through the lentils, removing any stones or seeds, then soak them in cold water for 1 hour. Drain the water then rinse the lentils well. Melt 15g/½oz of the butter in a pan, add the shallots and the diced bacon and fry for 1 minute. Add the lentils, then pour in the chicken stock, season with a few turns of pepper and add the bay leaf. Bring to the boil, cover the pan and cook in an oven heated to 220°C/425°F gas 7 for 45 minutes.

Heat the oil with 15g/½oz of the butter in an ovenproof pan large enough to take all of the partridges. Season the partridges well, then sear the birds over high heat on all sides, browning them well. Remove from the pan, add the mirepoix and brown lightly. Pour in the red wine and brown chicken stock. Add the thyme and garlic and bring it to the boil. Stand the partridges in the pan, cover and cook in an oven heated to 220°C/425F/gas 7 for 25 minutes. Once cooked, remove the birds and allow to rest in a warm place for 10 minutes. Pour the stock through a fine strainer and reduce over high heat until only about 200ml/7floz remains.

To Serve

Remove the legs and breasts from the partridges and return to the oven for about 2 minutes to reheat. Return the sauce to the boil then remove it from the heat. Gradually add the remaining butter, piece by piece, until it has melted. Divide the lentils evenly between the plates. Place 2 legs and 2 breasts on top of the lentils and pour the sauce around.

Roast Partridge with Calvados

Method

Remove the wish bones from the partridges and truss the birds (see pages 218–20). Lightly season the birds inside and out. Cut each slice of bacon in two and tie around the breasts.

Heat the oil with 15g/½oz of the butter in a roasting pan. Sear the birds in the hot fat on all sides. Place them on to one leg and roast in an oven heated to 230°C/450°F/gas 8 for 4 minutes. Turn the birds on to their other leg and continue roasting for a further 4 minutes. Turn the partridges on to their backs and finish cooking for a further 4 minutes. Once cooked, transfer them to a warm place to rest for about 10 minutes.

Peel the apples, cut into quarters and slice each quarter into three. Melt 15g/½oz of the butter in a frying pan, add the sliced apple, sprinkle with sugar and fry until golden brown. Remove from the pan and keep warm.

Remove the legs and the breasts from all of the birds, and keep them covered and warm. Roughly chop the carcasses and lightly brown in the roasting pan. Pour off the fat and pour in the Calvados, ignite it then pour in the stock. Reduce over high heat until only about 175ml/6floz remains.

To Serve

Return the partridges to the oven for 1 minute to reheat.

Pour the sauce through a fine strainer or muslin and return the sauce to the boil. Remove from the heat and gradually add the remaining butter, piece by piece, until it has melted. Divide the apple slices neatly between the plates. Place 2 legs on top of the apples then arrange the breasts on top of the legs. Pour the sauce over and around the partridge.

4 PORTIONS

4 partridges
salt and freshly ground white
   pepper
4 slices of streaky bacon
4 tsp oil
50g/2oz unsalted butter
3 eating apples
4 tsp caster sugar
120ml/4floz Calvados
300ml/½pt brown chicken or
   pheasant stock (see page
   198 or 200)

Roast Breast of Partridge with Crisply Fried Celeriac

4 PORTIONS
4 young partridges
4 slices of bacon, rinds
    removed
salt and freshly ground white
    pepper
oil for deep frying, plus 2 tsp
25g/1oz butter
150ml/¼pt dry white wine
1 tbsp fresh thyme leaves
450ml/¾pt game stock (see
    page 200)
½ celeriac, peeled and cut into
    fine strips

Method

Remove the legs from the partridges, chop them up and save to make the sauce. Truss the birds (see pages 218–20), lay the bacon over the breasts and tie with string. Season the partridges. Heat the 2 teaspoons of oil in a roasting pan, add the butter then seal the birds in the hot fat. Roast in an oven heated to 230°C/450°F/gas 8 for 9 minutes, turning every 3 minutes. Keep warm.

Pour off the fat from the roasting pan then brown the partridge legs. Add the wine and reduce over high heat until almost gone. Add two-thirds of the thyme along with the stock, bring to the boil then reduce until the sauce just starts to thicken. While the sauce is reducing, remove the breasts from the partridges and keep warm. Chop up the bones and add these to the sauce.

To Serve

Return the breasts to the oven for 2 minutes to reheat.

Heat the oil for deep-frying to 190°C/375°F. Quickly deep-fry the celeriac until golden brown. Drain on kitchen paper then season lightly with salt. Place a 12.5cm/5 inch pastry cutter in the centre of each plate. Place a quarter of the celeriac in this. Remove the cutter and sit 2 breasts on top. Strain the sauce through a fine strainer or muslin and add the remaining thyme. Spoon a little of the sauce over the breasts then pour the remainder on to the plates.

BREAST OF PARTRIDGE WITH BRAISED LETTUCE

Method

Remove the legs from each partridge, and chop off the ends of the carcasses. Skin each leg and remove all of the meat. Roughly chop the leg bones and carcasses, and put to one side for use later. Place the leg meat into a food processor with the salt and process until smooth. Add the egg white and mix until it stiffens. Rub this mixture through a fine strainer into a bowl set over ice. Gradually add the cream, stirring well each time. Using a little of the butter, lightly butter 4 oval or round 120ml/4floz moulds. Test the mousse by dropping a teaspoon of the mixture into boiling water. If it is too firm, add a little more cream and test again. Fill each mould with the mousse mixture and cover each one with buttered foil.

Remove any discoloured leaves from the lettuces and trim the stems. Wash each lettuce well without breaking it up. Plunge the lettuces into a saucepan of boiling water and simmer for 5 minutes. Transfer them to iced water.

Heat the oil in an ovenproof dish. Lightly season the partridges, inside and out. Add the remaining butter to the oil, and quickly brown the partridges in this on all sides. Remove from the pan. Add the vegetables and the chopped bones and quickly brown these. Pour in the white wine then the game stock. Bring to the boil, then remove it from the heat. Add the garlic and the herbs. Place the partridges in the dish, then carefully add the lettuces. Cover with a tight fitting lid and cook in an oven heated to 200°C/400°F/gas 6 for 15 minutes.

Cook the mousses in the oven at the same time in a bain-marie for 15 minutes. Once cooked, remove the partridges and the lettuces from the pan, spoon over a little of the cooking liquor, cover and keep them warm with the mousses. Strain the liquor through a fine strainer or muslin into a saucepan and reduce it until only about 175ml/6floz remains.

To Serve

Carefully remove each breast from the partridges, cut off the wing bone and trim each breast so that they are a neat shape. Place two breasts side by side on each plate at 6 o'clock. Cut each lettuce in two lengthways, and carefully arrange the leaves to make 8 neat parcels. Place one each side of the breasts. Remove the mousses from their moulds and place one on each plate at 12 o'clock. Spoon the sauce over and around the partridge breasts.

4 PORTIONS

4 partridges
½ tsp salt
1 egg white
150ml/¼pt double cream
20g/¾oz unsalted butter
4 small firm lettuces
2 tsp oil
salt and freshly ground white pepper
115g/4oz mirepoix (leek, onion, carrot and celery)
85ml/3floz dry white wine
250ml/9floz game stock (see page 200)
1 garlic clove, roughly chopped
1 bay leaf
1 sprig of fresh thyme

PHEASANT

French: *Faisan* German: *Fasan* Italian: *Fagiano*

It would be true to say that if shooting were ever banned, then the first quarry to be lost to our countryside would be the pheasant. For it is shooting alone that gives us this splendid highly coloured, most attractive of British birds. Saying the pheasant is British, however, is not strictly true. It is widely thought that it was brought to this country by the Romans, and that they were reared as domestic fowl, not as sporting birds. However, legend has it that the pheasant was first introduced into Europe by Jason and the Argonauts around 1300 BC.

By no means is the pheasant confined merely to Britain – it is to be found in large quantities from North America through to China and from Norway to New Zealand. Ask anyone, town dweller or countryman, to describe a pheasant and they will all give a fairly accurate description – it is by far the most easily recognized bird we have. The reason is simple. It is estimated that some 10 million pheasants are reared and released each year, and almost every excursion into the countryside will result in the sighting of at least one pheasant.

The culinary qualities of the pheasant are well known, with a gamey poultry flavour but a meatier, slightly drier texture than that of domestic fowl. I, along with many others, prefer the hen pheasant to its more colourful and much larger male counterpart, the hen having a slightly more delicate flavour and finer texture. Also for my purposes, the hen, being smaller, will yield two good portions whereas the cock is just a little too large. As with all game, care in cooking is most important as it will easily dry out.

Although pheasants are in season from the 1st of October to the 1st of February, very few are actually shot until late into November, as they are considered to be immature before then. I believe pheasant to be at its best in December and January, once the winter weather has really set in and the birds take on a little more fat!

Both the sexing and the ageing of the pheasant is relatively easy. The male pheasant, with its dark green head and red face, purple-chestnut and black iridescent body feathers and long magnificent tail is quite a contrast to the drab looking female with her chestnut and brown feathers with touches of black. A short rounded spur on the male can mean that it is a first year bird, or a long pointed spur that it is an old bird, but this is not always reliable. The best way to age a pheasant is to hold it by its bottom beak. If it supports its own weight without bending then it is old. If, however, the bottom beak bends then you have a young bird.

Undoubtedly, the pheasant is a magnificent bird, the cock proud and splendid in its fine plumage. Prepared for the table it is food for a king at a very modest price, and flying high and fast on a crisp winter's morning it is fabulous sport for a great many people.

Consommé of Pheasant Perfumed with Wild Mushrooms

Method

Chop the pheasant meat finely. Trim the field or cup mushrooms, removing any root and brushing off any dirt. Finely dice these along with the vegetables and herbs. Place in a saucepan with the meat and egg whites. Mix well. Stir in the cold stock, Madeira and salt and pepper. Place over high heat, stirring constantly until it almost comes to the boil. Just as it comes to the boil reduce the heat so that it just simmers. Simmer for 30 minutes. Pour through a muslin-lined strainer. If there is a thin film of fat on the top of the consommé, this can be removed by pulling a sheet of kitchen paper over the surface.

To Serve

Presoak the morels in cold water for at least 2 hours before needed. Trim the wild mushrooms of any root and brush off any dirt. Slice each of the cèpes into four. Return the consommé to the boil, add the wild mushrooms and allow them to sit in the consommé over a very low heat for 2 minutes. Ladle the consommé into soup plates and divide the wild mushrooms between them. Sprinkle a few parsley leaves on to the consommé before serving.

4 PORTIONS

1 pheasant leg, skinned and boned
85g/3oz field or cup mushrooms
½ stalk celery
½ small onion
25g/1oz leek
1 tomato
1 sprig of fresh thyme
few parsley stalks
2 egg whites
1l/1¾pt cold pheasant stock (see page 200)
25ml/1floz Madeira
salt and freshly ground white pepper
8 dried morels
2 small cèpes
8 small girolles
8 chanterelles
flat-leaved parsley, to garnish

*Terrine of Pheasant Rillettes
(see page 84)*

Terrine of Pheasant Rillettes

20–22 PORTIONS
5 pheasants
675g/1½lb lard
salt and freshly ground white
  pepper
450g/1lb large carrots, diced
6–8 large spinach leaves

TO SERVE
garlic vinaigrette (see page
  205)
blanched baby Brussels
  sprouts
wild cress

Method

Remove the legs and breasts from the pheasants (see pages 216–17). Skin and bone the legs and remove the skin from the breasts. Trim off any fat and remove the sinew from the breasts. Dice all the meat. Melt the lard. Season the meat with 4 teaspoons of salt and a little pepper and place in a saucepan. Pour over the lard – the meat should be completely covered. Stand the saucepan in a roasting pan half-filled with boiling water and simmer over low heat for 3–4 hours. The meat is cooked when it will easily fall apart.

Cook the carrots in boiling salted water until soft, refresh in cold water then drain. Set aside. Once the meat is cooked, drain off the fat. Allow to settle then skim off the fat and reserve. You should now have about 600ml/1pt of pheasant juice left. Set this over high heat and reduce by three-quarters. Once reduced, add to the pheasant meat along with the carrot and half of the reserved fat. Mix in well. Stand in a cold place and mix occasionally until it has almost set.

Press the mixture into an 28cm/11 inch terrine then place it in the refrigerator for 1 hour. Melt the remaining fat, less 50ml/2floz, and pour on top of the terrine – this will form an airtight seal. Chill until set.

To Finish

Remove the stalks from the spinach leaves and wash well. Blanch in boiling salted water for a few seconds and refresh under cold water. Dry the leaves well. Turn out the terrine by dipping the mould in hot water for about 30 seconds. Give it a sharp tap and it should fall out easily. Brush the terrine with a little of the reserved fat. Cover the terrine with the spinach leaves on the three long sides, brushing each with a little fat, leaving only the top where the fat was added uncovered. Leave to set.

To Serve

Cut the terrine into slices. Lay a slice in the centre of each plate, spoon a little garlic vinaigrette around it and finish with tiny Brussels sprouts and wild cress.

Sautéed Breast of Pheasant with Girolles, Foie Gras and Grapes

Method

Trim the pheasant breasts to remove excess fat but leave the skin on. Season. Carefully wipe the girolles clean to remove any dirt and grit – do not wash.

Heat the oil in a pan, add half the butter and when it sizzles add the breasts and cook gently on one side until lightly browned, turn and complete the cooking, again only browning lightly. When cooked the pheasant should still be slightly pink in the centre. If it is cooked any more than this it will be too dry.

Return the pan to the heat and add the girolles. Season lightly and fry gently until cooked. When almost cooked, add the grapes. Remove the grapes and mushrooms from the pan, cover and keep warm. Pour off the fat and add the white wine. Reduce over high heat until almost gone. Add the stock, bring to the boil and reduce until it starts to thicken. Strain through a fine strainer or muslin.

To Serve

Place the pheasant breasts in an oven heated to 220°C/425°F/gas 7 for about 1 minute to reheat.

Gradually whisk the remaining butter in to the sauce, piece by piece, until it has all melted. Season the diced foie gras. Heat a dry frying pan and quickly fry the foie gras for a couple of seconds, add the girolles and grapes and toss together until hot. Place a pile of the girolle mixture just off centre on each plate, slice each pheasant breast into 6 slices, and lay on the plate next to the girolles. Pour the sauce over and around the pheasant.

4 PORTIONS
4 pheasant breasts
salt and freshly ground white pepper
85g/3oz girolles
1 tbsp oil
50g/2oz cold unsalted butter, diced
150g/5oz seedless white grapes, peeled
85ml/3floz dry white wine
300ml/½pt pheasant stock (see page 200)
50g/2oz fresh foie gras, diced

Breast of Pheasant with Caramelized Apples and a Hint of Curry

I served this dish to a lunch party we had for friends: it must-have gone down well because they returned the following week to the restaurant and had it again, but this time they paid for it. A few weeks later I served the same dish again to my Saturday morning cookery class. Again, a couple returned the following week and ordered it. So with recommendations like that, can you afford not to try it?

4 PORTIONS

4 pheasant breasts

40g/1½oz unsalted butter

3 dessert apples, peeled, cored and diced

40g/1½oz sugar

salt and freshly ground white pepper

2 tsp oil

50ml/2floz dry white wine

175ml/6floz curry sauce (see page 202)

85ml/3floz double cream

4 tomatoes, skinned, seeded and diced

4 sprigs of fresh dill

Method

Melt 25g/1oz of the butter, add the apples and fry over high heat for 1 minute, tossing frequently. Add the sugar and fry, tossing the apples occasionally, until they are an even golden brown. Season the breasts. Heat the oil in another pan, add the remaining butter and, once sizzling, place the breasts skin side down into the pan. Cook over low heat for about 3 minutes on each side. Be careful not to over-cook them – pheasant is best left slightly pink as it dries out very quickly. Remove the breasts from the pan and keep warm. Pour off the fat from the pan, add the white wine and reduce until almost gone. Add the curry sauce and bring to the boil. Once boiling, add the cream and reduce slightly.

To Serve

Lightly season the tomatoes and either place a neat pile towards one edge of the plate, or alternatively press the tomato into a small pastry cutter to form four turrets. Reheat the apple in a frying pan. Slice the pheasant breasts and place in an oven heated to 220°C/425°F/gas 7 for about 1 minute to reheat. Place a bed of the apple on each plate the size and shape of a breast. Place a pheasant breast on each pile of apple, strain the sauce and pour around the plates. Finish with a sprig of fresh dill on each breast.

Breast of Pheasant with Caramelized Apples and a Hint of Curry

Breast of Pheasant with a Watercress and Potato Sauce

4 PORTIONS

4 pheasant breasts

115g/4oz watercress

20g/¾oz unsalted butter

1 shallot, finely chopped

salt and freshly ground white
    pepper

300ml/½pt chicken stock (see
    page 198)

1 tbsp oil

50ml/2floz dry white wine

150g/5oz potatoes, cut into
    1cm/½ inch dice

85ml/3floz double cream

Method

Trim each pheasant breast to remove any excess sinew and skin, leaving only a neat covering of skin and leaving the wing bone attached. Pick through the watercress, removing half of the stalk, then roughly chop. Melt half the butter in a saucepan, add the shallot and fry gently, without colouring, for about 20 seconds. Add the watercress and a little salt and pepper, and cook until it starts to soften. Pour in the chicken stock. Bring to the boil and simmer for 3 minutes. Transfer the sauce to a liquidizer and liquidize until smooth. Pour the sauce through a strainer.

Lightly season the breasts on both sides. Heat the oil with the remaining butter in a frying pan and place the breasts in, skin side down. Fry gently for 5 minutes then turn over and cook for a further 5 minutes. When cooked the breasts should still be a little pink inside. Transfer to a warm place to rest. Pour off the fat, then add the white wine. Reduce over high heat until almost gone. Pour in the watercress sauce and add the diced potato. Simmer until the potato is almost cooked. Pour in the cream and continue cooking until the potato is fully cooked. Keep the sauce warm.

To Serve

Place the pheasant breasts in an oven heated to 220°C/425°F/gas 7 for about 2 minutes to reheat. Once they are well warmed through, remove the wing bones from the breasts and slice each into 6 or 7 slices lengthways. Spoon the sauce on to the plates, arranging the potatoes in a rough circle. Fan a pheasant breast on to the sauce in the centre of each plate.

Breast of Pheasant 'En Papillote' with Wild Mushrooms

This is an extremely simple and effective way of cooking, ensuring that all the flavour and aroma is kept. The only trick is in efficiently sealing the bag. For luxury and flavour, try adding a little truffle juice instead of Madeira and a few strips or slices of truffle.

4 PORTIONS
4 pheasant breasts
225g/8oz mixed wild
   mushrooms (cèpes, girolles,
   chanterelles, pleurots)
25g/1oz butter
salt and freshly ground white
   pepper
4 sprigs of fresh thyme
4 tbsp Madeira
120ml/4floz pheasant stock
   (see page 200)

Method

Trim the pheasant breasts of any sinew and excess skin, leaving the wing bone on. Using a small sharp knife, remove any dirt and root from the mushrooms. Thickly slice the cèpes and cut the other mushrooms into even-sized pieces.

Take 4 sheets of greaseproof paper or foil about 25×30cm/10× 12 inches. Divide the butter into four and place a piece in the centre of one half of each sheet. Place the breasts on top of the butter and season them lightly. Divide the mushrooms evenly across the breasts, then place a sprig of thyme on top. Fold the paper over and seal two of the edges to form a bag, by rolling the paper over tightly to form a seal. Pour 1 tablespoon of the Madeira into each bag along with one-quarter of the stock. Seal the remaining open edge of each bag. Place on to a baking tray and cook in an oven heated to 230°C/ 450°F/gas 8 for 12–14 minutes, depending upon whether they are hen or cock pheasants – hens are smaller.

To Serve

Either transfer the unopened bags to warmed serving plates and serve them immediately while they are still inflated, letting your guests experience breaking their own bag open and the wonderful aroma that wafts out. Or, open each bag in the kitchen and transfer the contents to the plates, being careful to arrange them neatly.

Breast of Pheasant with Rillettes of Its Legs and a Rich Armagnac Sauce (see page 92)

Breast of Pheasant with Rillettes of Its Legs and a Rich Armagnac Sauce

4 PORTIONS
2 pheasants
¾ tsp salt
1 garlic clove
175g/6oz lard
25g/1oz sultanas
120ml/4floz Armagnac
salt and freshly ground white
    pepper
2 tsp oil
15g/½oz unsalted butter
350ml/12floz pheasant stock
    (see page 200)
4 sprigs of fresh dill

Method

Remove the legs from the pheasants. Take out the wish bone and remove the breasts (see pages 216–17). Trim the breasts of any sinew and excess skin, leaving a neat covering of skin and the wing bones on. Skin the legs and remove the thigh meat. Sprinkle the thigh meat with ¾ teaspoon of salt then leave it to stand in the refrigerator for 24 hours.

Place the garlic and lard in a saucepan and melt over gentle heat. Add the pieces of pheasant thigh and cook them slowly in the fat in a bain-marie for 4 hours. When cooked the meat should fall apart easily. Drain the meat from the fat and discard the garlic. Rub the meat between your fingers to break it into small fibres. Save one-third of the fat for later and mix the remaining fat into the meat. Allow it to almost set, stirring occasionally.

Transfer the meat to a container, pressing it in well. The container should be large enough to make a layer of meat about 4cm/1½ inches deep. Pour the reserved fat on top and chill until set. Soak the sultanas in the Armagnac for at least 2 hours.

Lightly season the pheasant breasts on both sides. Heat the oil in a frying pan with the butter and fry the breasts for 5 minutes on each side, starting with the skin side down. When cooked the breasts should still be slightly pink in the centre. Transfer to a warm place to rest. Pour off the fat from the pan, add the Armagnac from the sultanas and reduce by two-thirds. Pour in the stock and reduce this by half.

To Serve

Place the pheasant breasts in an oven heated to 220°C/420°F/gas 7 for about 2 minutes to reheat.

Strain the sauce through a fine strainer or muslin on to the sultanas and keep warm. Using a 4cm/1½ inch round cutter cut out 4 rounds from the rillette. Cut each pheasant breast into two horizontally, starting at the point of the breast and stopping just before the wing bone. Spoon a little of the sauce on to the centre of each plate, fan a breast on to this, and spoon the remaining sauce over the breasts. Place a rillette at about 11 o'clock on each plate and finish the dish with a sprig of dill draped over each breast.

QUAIL
French: *Caille* German: *Wachtel* Italian: *Quaglia*

Although quail is not strictly poultry – more like domestic game really –
it has been bred domestically for 4000 years. It is probably the only
game bird that has so far seemed amenable to domestication, as all the
groundwork was done all those years ago in Japan, where they were
inexplicably kept as song birds (if you have ever heard the 'song' of the
quail, you will understand my misgivings). They are still to be found in
the wild in some countries – Spain, southern France, north Africa and
the Middle East – but it is really only in North America that they are
found in any numbers and are still regarded as a quarry species.

The Japanese quail is the species bred for its culinary attributes and is
farmed throughout the world. Although most commercial producers of
quail probably sell them at 6 weeks, I, and my supplier, believe they are
at their best at 8 weeks, by which time they have started to fill out and
achieve a light fat covering. The best weight I find is a bird weighing
between 125–150g/4½–5oz, preferably female, as they tend to have a
slightly higher proportion of meat than their male counterparts. The male
on the other hand has a redeeming feature that the female does not
possess, *rognon du coq* – testicles. Escoffier refers to them in numerous
recipes as a garnish, and keeps referring to them as small. In relation to
the size of the bird they are anything *but* small – well-endowed I think is
the term! Of course, the quail also produces a delightful egg, of immense
size and pretty pattern which is considered to be a great delicacy. But
more about this in the chapter on eggs (see pages 168–76).

Consommé of Quail garnished with Its Eggs Poached and Its Breast sliced

4 PORTIONS
6 quails
1 stalk celery
1 small onion
1 carrot
50g/2oz leek
1 tsp oil
1.2l/2¼pt chicken stock (see page 198)
1 sprig of thyme
½ garlic clove
1 bay leaf
1 tomato
4 sprigs of coriander
2 egg whites
salt and freshly ground white pepper
8 quails' eggs
2 tsp vinegar
12 coriander leaves

Method

Remove the legs from all of the quails. Remove the breast meat from 3 of the quails (see pages 216–17), cover and leave it in the refrigerator until later. Chop off the end of the carcass from 2 of the quails and remove the first 2 parts of the wings. Set these 2 double quail breasts aside for later. Roughly chop the remaining quail along with all of the legs and the bones. Rinse in cold water and dry well.

Roughly chop half the celery, carrot and leek. Heat the oil in a frying pan, add the chopped quail and carcasses and fry over high heat until lightly browned. Add the chicken stock and just as it starts to come to the boil, skim off any fat and scum on the surface. Add the thyme, garlic and bay leaf, and simmer very slowly for 1 hour. Plunge in the 2 reserved double quail breasts and allow these to cook for 10 minutes. Once cooked, remove the breasts and allow them to cool. When the stock is ready, strain it through a fine strainer and allow it to go cold.

To clarify the consommé, finely chop the remaining vegetables along with the tomato, coriander sprigs, and the reserved quail meat. Put in a saucepan along with the egg whites and mix together well. Stir in the cold stock and check the mixture for seasoning. Bring to the boil over high heat, stirring continuously until it almost comes to the boil. Just as it comes to the boil, reduce the heat so that it simmers. Continue simmering for 30 minutes. Strain the finished consommé through muslin. If there is a thin film of fat on the top of the consommé, this can be removed by pulling a sheet of kitchen paper across the surface.

To Serve

Poach the quails' eggs in water with the vinegar, then drop them into iced water to cool. Using a small knife, carefully remove the breasts from the poached quail, remove the skin and slice each breast into about 6 slices across and at a slight angle. Reheat the consommé. Place 2 eggs and a sliced breast into each soup plate, pour the consommé into the plates, and finish with 3 coriander leaves floating on top of each bowl.

Consommé of Quail with Its Eggs Poached and Its Breast Sliced

Warm Salad of Quail, Quails' Eggs and Toasted Pine Kernels

4 PORTIONS

4 quails

salt and freshly ground white
    pepper

1 tbsp oil

15g/½oz unsalted butter

15g/½oz pine kernels

¼ head curly endive

¼ head red oak leaf lettuce

½ small head raddichio

25g/1oz corn salad

1 tbsp walnut oil

8 quails' eggs

Method

If the quails still have their livers, then leave them. Truss the quails (see pages 218–20) and season lightly. Heat half the oil in a roasting pan. Add half the butter and, once sizzling, quickly sear the quails on all sides. Place each quail on one leg and roast in an oven heated to 230°C/450°F/gas 8 for 4 minutes. Turn each quail on to the other leg and roast for a further 4 minutes. Turn them on to their backs, baste, and cook for a final 4 minutes. Leave to rest and cool. Toast the pine kernels either under a hot grill or in the oven until golden brown. Pick through the salad leaves, wash well and dry.

To Serve

Joint each quail into legs and breasts. Remove all the bones. If the livers were in the bird then carefully remove them and trim off the gall bladders. Keep warm. Lightly season the lettuce leaves, add the walnut oil and toss well. Return all the pieces of quail to the oven for about 1 minute to reheat. Arrange the salad leaves in a circle on the plates. Heat the remaining oil and butter in a small frying pan and gently fry the quails' eggs in pairs. Arrange 2 quail breasts and 2 legs and their livers on each plate, and place a pair of fried eggs in the centre of each plate. Season the eggs with salt and sprinkle over the pine kernels.

Note

The cooking time for the quail assumes they are medium to large, weighing between 125–150g/4½–5oz. If they are smaller, then 3 minutes per side should be sufficient.

Warm Salad of Roast Quail, Shallots and Red Cabbage

Method

Cut the red cabbage into quarters, remove the core and very finely slice the leaves and the onion. Mix the cabbage and onion together then season with the salt, a little pepper and sugar. Add the walnut and salad oils and vinegar and mix well. Leave to stand for at least 24 hours.

Heat half of the oil and half of the butter in a small roasting pan. Lightly season the quails then sear them on all sides in the hot fat. Lay them on one leg and roast in an oven heated to 230°C/450°F/gas 8 for 3 minutes, turn on to the other leg and roast for a further 3 minutes. Turn on to their backs, baste well and roast for a further 4 minutes. Keep warm.

Pour off the fat from the pan. Heat the remaining oil and butter in the pan until it sizzles. Roast the shallots in this for about 8 minutes, turning them occasionally. Keep warm. Remove the legs and the breasts from the quails and keep warm. Roughly chop the carcasses. Pour off most of the fat from the pan. Quickly fry the carrot, celery, garlic and quail carcasses over high heat until lightly browned. Pour in the white wine and reduce until almost gone. Add the stock and thyme and reduce this by about half. Strain through a fine strainer or muslin.

To Serve

Return the quails and roasted shallots to the oven for about 1 minute to reheat.

Drain the red cabbage and arrange it on the plates in a loose nest. Place 2 legs in the centre of each nest with 2 breasts on top. Arrange the shallots around the edge and pour the sauce on to the plates.

4 PORTIONS

4 quails
1 small red cabbage, weighing about 350g/12oz
1 small onion
salt and freshly ground white pepper
2 tsp sugar
4 tbsp walnut oil
4 tbsp salad oil
5 tbsp sherry vinegar
2 tsp oil for frying
25g/1oz butter
20 shallots
1 small carrot, chopped
1 stalk celery, chopped
½ garlic clove, chopped
25ml/1floz dry white wine
225ml/8floz brown chicken stock (see page 198)
2 sprigs of fresh thyme

Roast Quail with a Salad of Quails' Eggs and Crayfish Tails

4 PORTIONS

2 × 150g/5oz quails
8 quails' eggs
2 tsp oil
50g/2oz unsalted butter, diced
20 live crayfish
85ml/3floz fish stock (see page 199)
50ml/2floz dry sherry
1 small carrot, finely sliced
1 shallot, finely sliced
lettuce leaves (curly endive, corn salad, raddichio, red oak leaf)
2 tsp double cream
2 tbsp vinaigrette dressing
2 tsp chopped chives
sprigs of fresh dill, to garnish

Method

Poach the quails' eggs for 3 minutes and refresh in cold water when cooked. Roast the quails in the oil and about 15g/½oz of the butter in an oven heated to 230°C/450°F/gas 8 for 10 minutes – 3 minutes on each leg and 4 minutes on their backs. Remove from the pan and leave to rest and cool.

Remove the intestinal tract from the crayfish by pinching the middle section of the tail between your thumb and forefinger, then twist and pull. Discard the fat from the roasting pan, add the fish stock and dry sherry and bring to the boil. When boiling, plunge in the crayfish and cover with a lid. Cook the crayfish for 3 minutes, remove from the pan and drain. Add the carrot and shallot to the liquid and continue boiling until it is syrupy. Meanwhile, remove the tail meat from the crayfish (save the shells as they are very good in a sauce or soup). Pick through the lettuce leaves, wash them well and dry thoroughly.

To Serve

Remove the legs and breasts from the quails, and reheat in the oven. When the sauce is ready, add the cream and bring back to the boil, then add the crayfish tails. Remove from the heat and gradually whisk in the remaining butter, piece by piece, until all the butter has melted. Arrange the lettuce leaves on the plates, place two eggs on each plate and spoon over the vinaigrette. Top with the chopped chives. Divide the quail meat among the plates, allowing 1 leg and 1 breast each, and add the crayfish and sauce. Garnish with sprigs of fresh dill.

Roast Quail on a Bed of Wild rice with a Sauce of Black Truffles

Method

Wash the rice two or three times in clean, cold water. Add it to the chicken stock with a pinch of salt. Bring it to the boil and simmer gently for 1 hour. Remove the wish bones from the quails, and truss them (see pages 218–20). Heat the oil in a roasting pan and add 15g/½oz of the butter. Lightly season the quails and quickly sear them on all sides in the hot fat. Place them on to one leg and roast in an oven heated to 230°C/450°F/gas 8 for 3 minutes. Turn them on to the other leg and roast for a further 3 minutes. Turn on to their backs and roast for a final 4 minutes. Remove from the pan and allow them to rest in a warm place for at least 10 minutes.

Remove the legs and breasts from each quail, cut off the drumsticks and remove the bones from the thighs. Cover the thigh and the breast meat and keep warm. Roughly chop the carcasses and the drumsticks. Melt about 10g/¼oz of the remaining butter in a pan and quickly and lightly brown the bones. Pour in the Madeira and reduce it slightly. Pour in the brown chicken stock and simmer for about 10 minutes. Pour the sauce through a strainer or muslin on to the diced truffle and reduce this until only 225ml/8floz remains.

To Serve

Return the quails to the oven for about 1 minute to reheat.

Drain the rice and gently reheat in the remaining butter. Place about 4 tablespoons of the rice on to each plate, one at 12 o'clock, one at 3 o'clock, one at 6 and one at 9. On each pile place a thigh topped with a breast, spoon the sauce on to the plates and a little over each breast.

4 PORTIONS

8 quails
115g/4oz wild rice
600ml/1pt chicken stock (see page 198)
salt and freshly ground white pepper
2 tsp oil
35g/1¼oz unsalted butter
120ml/4floz Madeira
350ml/12floz brown chicken stock (see page 198)
25g/1oz black truffle, cut into 3mm/⅛ inch dice

Roast Quail with Grapes and a Honey Sauce

4 PORTIONS

8 quails

24 muscat grapes

50g/2oz watercress

salt and freshly ground white
    pepper

2 tsp oil

20g/4oz unsalted butter

2 shallots, finely diced

1 tbsp honey

85ml/3floz dry white wine

350ml/12floz brown chicken
    stock (see page 198)

8 small tartlet cases,
    approximately 5cm/2 inches
    in diameter

Method

Remove the wish bones from the quails and truss them (see pages 218–20). Peel the grapes and carefully remove the seeds, leaving the grapes whole. Pick the watercress to remove their stalks, wash the leaves and drain them well.

Lightly season the quail. Heat the oil and 15g/½oz of the butter in a roasting tray. Quickly sear the quails on all sides in the hot fat, browning lightly. Place them on to one leg and then into an oven heated to 230°C/450°F/gas 8 to roast for 3 minutes. Turn the birds on to their other leg and continue roasting for a further 3 minutes. Turn them on to their backs and roast for a final 4 minutes. Once cooked, remove the birds from the oven and allow to rest in a warm place for 10 minutes. Once rested, remove the legs and breasts from each quail and keep them warm. Roughly chop the carcasses. Tip the fat from the pan, add the chopped shallots and the honey and over medium heat allow these to caramelize slightly, stirring often. Pour in the white wine and reduce until almost gone. Pour in the stock, add the chopped carcasses and simmer and reduce until only about 225ml/8floz remains.

To Serve

Return the quails to the oven along with the tartlet cases for 2 minutes to reheat. Strain the sauce through a fine strainer or muslin on to the grapes and keep warm. Melt the remaining butter in a saucepan until it sizzles, then add the watercress. Season lightly and cook the watercress until soft. Once cooked, drain and divide it out evenly between the tartlet cases. Drain the grapes from the sauce and place 3 in each case on top of the watercress. Place 1 quail, legs crossed on the bottom and 2 breasts on top, at 12 o'clock on each plate and 1 quail at 6 o'clock. Pour the sauce over and around the quails. Place 2 tartlet cases on each plate, 1 at 3 o'clock and 1 at 9 o'clock and serve immediately.

Galantine of Quail on a Salad of Mange-tout

Method

Carefully remove the bones from six of the quails, leaving the birds as whole as possible, but leaving the leg bones in. The easiest way of doing this is, using a small sharp pointed knife, make an incision along the back from the neck to the point where the legs join the body. Carefully work your way around the carcass.

Remove the skin from the remaining bird and discard. Remove all the meat and roughly chop. Place this with ½ teaspoon of salt in a food processor and process until smooth. Add the egg white and process until it stiffens. Rub this mixture through a fine strainer into a bowl set over crushed ice. Gradually add the cream, mixing it in well but being careful not to overbeat. Stir in the chopped truffle and pistachios. Test the mousse by dropping a teaspoon of the mixture into boiling water. If it is too firm, add a little more cream and test again.

Lay the quails skin side down on the work surface and lightly season. Divide the mousse between the quails and carefully form each one back into its original shape, making sure the mousse is completely enclosed. Wrap each bird in cling film to preserve the shape and twist the ends. Drop into boiling water, cover and simmer gently for 25 minutes. Once cooked, drop into iced water. Drain and chill for 24 hours.

Roughly chop the quail carcasses. Heat the cooking oil in a frying pan and brown the bones. Pour off the fat and add the stock. Simmer until reduced by half. Pour the stock through a fine strainer or muslin and leave to go cold.

Top and tail the mange-tout, blanch in boiling salted water until cooked but still slightly crisp. Refresh in cold water and drain.

To Serve

About 1 hour before serving, remove the quails from the cling film. Wipe each quail to remove any fat. Lightly brush each bird with the stock, which should be cold and on the point of setting. This will give the birds a glorious rich brown glaze. You may find it necessary to repeat this process two or three times so that the glaze is even. Return the birds to the refrigerator between each coat. Once glazed, carve 3 slices from each quail. Wash the lettuce leaves and dry well. In a bowl, mix the mange-tout with the shallot, a little salt and pepper and the olive oil. Place a lettuce leaf at 12 o'clock on each plate. Spoon the mange-tout salad into the centre. Place a quail, half on the lettuce leaf, and half on the mange-tout, laying the slices so they are running out from the main body.

6 PORTIONS

7 quails
½ tsp salt
1 egg white
120ml/4floz double cream
15g/½oz black truffle, cut into 3mm/⅛ inch dice
15g/½oz pistachio nuts, skinned and roughly chopped
2 tsp oil
175ml/6floz brown chicken stock (see page 198)
85g/3oz small mange-tout
1 shallot, finely chopped
salt and freshly ground white pepper
1 tbsp olive oil
4 leaves red oak leaf lettuce

Galantine of Quail on a Salad
of Mange-tout (see page 101)

SNIPE

French: *Bécassine* German: *Schnepfe* Italian: *Beccaccino*

As yet this magnificent little bird, the smallest game bird the British sportsman has on his quarry list, has never been farmed or reared, and probably never will be. Although snipe as a quarry are very limited in numbers, their addition to a shooter's game bag is highly prized. They are also rarely offered for sale as once shot they are normally the prerogative of the shooter. Consequently, I have given only a few recipes in this section, but any recipe for woodcock (see pages 120–5) will serve equally well with snipe.

There are many sub-species of snipe around the Northern Hemisphere wherever there is a suitable boggy marsh-type environment. The highly effective camouflage of the snipe makes it very difficult to spot and its erratic zig-zagging low flight makes for very difficult and exciting shooting. Its plumage is similar in colour to that of the woodcock, its nearest relative, except that the markings are arranged more in stripes, and its belly is almost white. It too has a long bill from which in most languages it derives its name. In season from the 12th of August until the 31st of January, this winged delicacy is at its best during the latter colder part of the season when it will be much plumper and more succulent. The snipe is considerably smaller than the woodcock, and where one woodcock will suffice, two snipe will be needed.

ROAST SNIPE WITH THYME

Method

If preparing yourself, carefully pluck the snipe, including the head and neck, taking care not to break the skin as it is very delicate, then singe (see page 214). Remove the insides, discarding the gizzard but keeping the entrails. Cut off the nails of each toe then truss the bird as for woodcock, twisting the head around and using its beak like a skewer, pushed through the thighs to hold the bird in shape. Wrap the legs of each bird in foil to prevent them from burning.

Peel the potatoes and, using either a mandolin or by hand, cut the potato into fine strips. Season the potato and mix it with the clarified butter. Heat a frying pan, divide the potato into 4 equal piles in the pan and form each one into a cake about 5cm/2 inches in diameter and 3mm/⅛ inch thick. Fry gently until golden brown on both sides. Remove from the pan and keep warm.

Lightly season each bird. Heat the oil with the butter in a roasting pan, and sear the birds over high heat for about 2 minutes on all sides. Place the birds on to their backs and roast in an oven heated to 240°C/475°F/gas 9 for 4 minutes. Once cooked, remove the birds from the oven and allow them to rest in a warm place for 5 minutes. Once rested, cut off the necks and remove the heads. Cut out the back bone from each bird and roughly chop these along with the necks. Cover the birds and keep them warm. Pour off the fat from the roasting pan and place over high heat. Add the chopped bones, the entrails and the shallot and brown lightly. Pour in the red wine and reduce by three-quarters. Pour in the stock and reduce by almost half.

To Serve

Return the snipe to the oven for about 1 minute to reheat.

Pour the sauce through a fine strainer or muslin on to the thyme and allow it to infuse for a minute. Place two potato cakes side by side on each plate with a snipe on top of each one. Pour the sauce around the potato cakes, and a little over the snipe.

2 PORTIONS
4 snipe
225g/8oz large potatoes
salt and freshly ground white pepper
20g/¾floz clarified butter (see page 208)
2 tsp oil
10g/¼oz unsalted butter
1 shallot, roughly chopped
85ml/3floz red wine
225ml/8floz brown chicken stock (see page 198)
1 tsp fresh thyme leaves

Roast Snipe on a Bed of Crisp Cabbage with Bacon and Sage

2 PORTIONS
4 snipe
50g/2oz streaky bacon
150g/5oz green winter cabbage
salt and freshly ground white
    pepper
2 tsp oil
10g/¼oz unsalted butter
1 shallot, roughly chopped
85ml/3floz red wine
225ml/8floz brown chicken
    stock (see page 198)
oil for deep-frying
12 fresh sage leaves, shredded

Method

If preparing yourself, carefully pluck the snipe, including the head and neck, taking care not to break the skin as it is very delicate, then singe (see page 214). Remove the insides, discarding the gizzard but keeping the entrails. Cut off the nails of each toe then truss the bird as for woodcock, by twisting the head around and using its beak like a skewer, pushed through the thighs to hold the bird in shape. Wrap the legs of each bird in foil to prevent them for burning. Cut the bacon into fine dice, plunge into boiling water for 30 seconds, then drain and allow to cool. Remove any stalk from the cabbage then shred the leaves.

Lightly season each bird. Heat the oil with the butter in a roasting pan, and sear the birds over high heat for about 2 minutes on all sides. Place the birds on to their backs and roast in an oven heated to 240°C/475°F/gas 9 for 4 minutes. Once cooked, remove the birds from the oven and allow them to rest in a warm place for 5 minutes. Once rested, cut off the necks and remove the heads. Cut the back bone from each bird and roughly chop these along with the necks. Cover the birds and keep them warm. Pour off the fat from the roasting pan and place over high heat. Add the chopped bones, the entrails and the shallot and brown lightly. Pour in the red wine and reduce by three-quarters. Pour in the stock and reduce this by almost half.

To Serve

Return the snipe to the oven for about 1 minute to reheat.

Deep-fry the shredded cabbage in hot fat for about 30 seconds, drain on kitchen paper and keep warm. Fry the diced bacon in a pan until crisp. Pour the sauce through a fine strainer or muslin on to the bacon and add the shredded sage. Arrange a pile of cabbage in the centre of each plate like a nest. Place 2 snipe on to each nest and spoon the sauce and garnish around the cabbage.

WILD DUCK
French: *Canard sauvage* German: *Wildente* Italian: *Anitra selvatica*

Although the term wild duck encompasses, amongst others, mallard, wigeon, teal and pintail, it is more generally used to describe the mallard. The other species, when offered for sale or on a restaurant menu, are generally referred to by their names.

The mallard is the most prolific of all the ducks and the most recognizable. It is also the only duck reared for sport. By far the largest of all the ducks, the male, as usual, is the most brightly coloured. Although its body is mainly grey with black and white at its rear, its head is a rich bottle green with a white ring on the neck and a yellowish bill. The breast is a rusty colour. Its wings have bands of royal blue, bottle green and white and black. By contrast, the female is very brown, mottled with black and orange.

The wigeon is a little smaller than the mallard and is easily distinguished by its chestnut brown head and neck, a yellowish forehead and a blue-grey bill with a black tip.

Teal is probably the tastiest of all the ducks, but I'm sure many people wonder if such a small bird is actually worth eating, as it really is tiny by comparison to the other species. It is a very pretty little bird, with a rich, cream-coloured breast speckled with black. The chestnut head has a sort of metallic green around the eyes running to the back of its neck. The female is, again, brown, with a white breast and belly.

The pintail is about the same size as the mallard, slightly smaller but larger than the wigeon. It is also quite a rare bird.

All these species are found throughout Europe and North America, as far north as Iceland, and, during severe winters, as far south as North Africa. I have only given recipes for mallard and teal in this section as they are the only ducks shot in any great numbers and are therefore more readily available. Recipes for mallard or teal will suit any species of wild duck. All these species of duck are in season from the 1st of September to the 31st of January inland, and to the 20th of February below the high water mark.

GALANTINE OF TEAL WITH A SALAD OF GIROLLES

4 PORTIONS

2 teal

25g/1oz pork fat

salt and freshly ground white pepper

½ recipe for panada (see page 207)

85ml/3floz double cream

1 tbsp Madeira

15g/½oz truffle, finely diced

1 tsp oil

50g/2oz mirepoix (mixed diced shallot, celery, leek and carrot)

175ml/6floz brown chicken stock (see page 198)

85g/3oz fresh girolles

2 tbsp salad oil

25ml/1floz red wine vinegar

2 handfuls mixed salad leaves (red oak leaf lettuce, corn salad, curly endive, lollo rosso)

Fiddly and long-winded this recipe may be, but worthwhile it certainly is. Not your everyday dinner dish, but it really will make an impressive first course for that special dinner party. The galantines should be made the day before eating but will keep for up to 4 days in the refrigerator once made.

Method

Reserve and chill the livers from the teal. Lay each bird, breast side down, on a work surface and, using a small sharp pointed knife, make an incision along the back from the neck to the parson's nose. Carefully work your way around the carcass freeing the meat from the bone, cutting through the wing bone and leg joints where they join the main body.

Once the main carcass has been removed, cut around the wing joints to free the meat and pull the bones out. Remove the leg bones. Save the bones. Being very careful not to break the skin, remove the meat from the legs and the wings, leaving only the breast meat in place. Remove the fillets from the breasts and put them with the leg meat. Using a sharp knife, cut a horizontal slice off each breast and place these on the skin above the breasts to extend the meat covering the skin. Chill for 1 hour.

Roughly chop the leg, wing and fillet meat and the pork fat. Chill along with the livers. Once cold, place it all into a food processor with ½ teaspoon of salt and a few turns of pepper and process until smooth. Add the panada and process again. Rub through a sieve, put into a bowl and chill well. Place the bowl over a bowl full of ice. Gradually add the cream and Madeira.

It is essential to test-cook a little of the finished mousse before using, for flavour and texture. Drop a teaspoon of the mixture into simmering water and cook for 1–2 minutes. Taste and adjust the seasoning as necessary. If the mousse is a little too firm then add a little more cream and re-test. Stir the truffle into the mousse.

Lay each teal, skin side down, on the work surface. Divide the mousse evenly down the centre of each bird and roll each teal into an even, thick roll making sure that the mousse is totally enclosed. Wrap each teal in cling film to preserve the shape and tie the ends. Place the galantines into simmering water and poach for 30 minutes. Do not allow the water to boil – the ideal temperature is 80°C/176°F. Anything above this and the texture of the galantines will become very grainy. Remove the pan from the heat and allow to go cold in the water. Once cold, drain and chill for 24 hours.

Roughly chop the bones and brown lightly in a teaspoon of the oil. Add the mirepoix and brown lightly. Tip off the fat and pour in the chicken stock. Simmer for about 15 minutes, until reduced by half. Strain through a fine strainer or muslin.

To Serve

Once the galantines are well chilled remove their cling film. Wipe each galantine to remove any surface fat. Lightly brush each galantine with half the stock which should be cold and on the point of setting. This will give the galantines a rich brown glaze. You may find it necessary to repeat this process two or three times so that the glaze is even. Return the galantines to the refrigerator between coats.

Trim the girolles of any root and brush off any dirt. Heat a little of the salad oil in a pan, add the girolles and cook for 30 seconds. Add the red wine vinegar and reduce it until almost gone. Pour in the remaining stock and simmer the girolles for 1 minute. Leave to go cold. Whisk in the remaining salad oil.

Tear the salad leaves into small pieces, wash and drain well. Cut each galantine into 6 slices, discarding the ends. Place 3 slices in a line down the centre of each plate. Drain the girolles from the sauce, lightly season the leaves and toss them with the sauce. Arrange the leaves neatly on the plates around the sliced galantine. Scatter the girolles around and spoon any excess sauce on to the plates.

Warm Salad of Teal with Cèpes

4 PORTIONS

2 teal
225g/8oz fresh cèpes
salt and freshly ground white
    pepper
2 tsp cooking oil
25g/1oz butter
85g/3oz mirepoix (leek, celery,
    shallot, carrot)
120ml/4floz red wine vinegar
150ml/¼pt brown chicken
    stock (see page 198)
½ garlic clove, roughly
    chopped
1 sprig of fresh thyme
50g/2oz corn salad
25ml/1floz walnut oil
40ml/1½floz olive oil

At first sight you may be forgiven for wondering whether this tiny little duck is actually worth the effort – believe me it most certainly is. Next to the woodcock I think it must be the finest game bird there is.

Method

Cut the legs off from the teal and remove the parson's nose end of the carcasses. Roughly chop the legs and set aside. Remove any root from the cèpes and wipe off any dirt. Thinly slice them and set to one side. Lightly season the teal both inside and out. Heat the oil in a roasting pan, add half of the butter and sear the teal on all sides until lightly browned. Roast in an oven heated to 240°C/475°F/gas 9 for 8 minutes. Transfer them to a warm place to rest for about 10 minutes. Remove both breasts from each teal and keep warm.

Roughly chop the carcasses and brown with the chopped legs in the roasting pan over high heat. When almost ready, add the mirepoix and brown this lightly. Pour off the fat, pour in the red wine vinegar and reduce until almost gone. Pour in the stock, add the garlic and thyme and reduce until only 50ml/2floz remains. Pour through a fine strainer or muslin.

To Serve

Wash and drain the corn salad and neatly arrange the leaves to cover the plates. Remove the skin from the teal breasts and slice each breast into as many thin slices as possible. Keep warm. Melt the remaining butter in a frying pan and, as soon as it starts to sizzle, add the sliced cèpes, lightly season them and quickly fry until only just cooked. Whisk the oils into the stock and gently warm it through, but do not allow it to get too hot. Spoon the cèpes into the centre of each plate. Lay the slices of teal over the cèpes and pour the warm dressing over the teal and the salad. Serve at once.

Warm Salad of Teal with Cèpes

BREAST OF WILD DUCK WITH CREAMED LEEKS AND A RICH PORT SAUCE

4 PORTIONS
2 wild ducks
salt and freshly ground white
    pepper
4 tsp oil
25g/1oz unsalted butter
85ml/3floz red wine
150ml/¼pt port
300ml/½pt veal stock (see page
    201)
225g/8oz leeks, diced
50ml/2floz double cream

Method

Remove the legs and the parson's nose end of the carcass from the ducks. Remove the wish bone, season the birds inside and out and truss (see pages 218–20). Skin the legs and roughly chop these along with the carcass. Heat half the oil in a roasting pan then add 15g/½oz of the butter. Sear the ducks on all sides in the hot fat until lightly browned. Place them on one breast and roast in an oven heated to 240°C/475°F/gas 9 for 5 minutes. Turn on to the other breast and roast for a further 5 minutes. Turn the ducks on to their backs and continue roasting for a further 5 minutes. Leave to rest in a warm place for 10 minutes.

Remove the breasts from the ducks and keep warm. Roughly chop the carcasses. Heat the remaining oil in a frying pan and add all the bones and the chopped legs, and brown well. Pour off the fat from the pan and add the red wine. Reduce until almost gone. Add the port and stock, and reduce this until only 225ml/8floz remains. Pour the sauce through a fine strainer or muslin.

To Serve

Melt the remaining butter in a saucepan, add the leeks and seasoning. Cook stirring often until soft. Once the leeks are almost done, pour in the cream. Bring to the boil and reduce until it thickens. Return the duck breasts to the oven for 2 minutes to reheat. Place a pool of the creamed leeks in an oval shape the size of the duck breasts in the centre of each plate. Pour the sauce around this. Remove the wing bone from each breast and carve into 6 slices across and at a slight angle. Lay a breast, slightly fanned, on top of the creamed leek.

AIR-DRIED WILD DUCK WITH A SALAD OF BABY VEGETABLES

Although curing and drying the duck takes over 2 weeks, it is very simple and the finished dish is not only a feast for the eyes and the palette, but also very unusual. Ordinary duck breasts can be used instead of wild duck.

Method

Mix together the salt, peppercorns, bay leaves, clove and the juniper berries. Sprinkle one-third of this on to a plate. Lay the duck breasts on this, skin side down, and cover the meat with the remaining salt mixture. Chill for 24 hours. After 24 hours brush off all the salt mixture, wrap each breast in muslin and hang them in a slightly draughty place at room temperature for 14 days to dry.

To Serve

Peel the carrots and turnips, leaving on about 1cm/½ inch of their green tops. Cut the fennel stalk into batons about 5cm/2 inches long. Place all the vegetables in a saucepan, except the fennel. Pour in the oil and the chicken stock, along with a little salt and pepper. Cover the pan with a lid and bring to the boil, then simmer gently until the vegetables are almost cooked – about 3 minutes. Add the fennel and the vinegar and continue cooking for a further minute. Leave to go cold.

Arrange the curly endive neatly on the plates, with the vegetables placed attractively through the leaves. Using a very sharp thin-bladed knife, remove the dark hard outer crust from the breasts. Cut each breast into very thin, long slices (about 14–16 from each breast). Arrange the slices over and through the salad. Spoon over the vegetable cooking stock and sprinkle the finished dish with the sprigs of chervil.

4 PORTIONS
2 wild duck breasts, trimmed of excess fat with wing bones removed
50g/2oz coarse salt
10g/¼oz black peppercorns, crushed
2 bay leaves, crushed
1 clove, crushed
4 juniper berries, crushed
12 baby carrots
12 baby turnips
1 stalk fennel
12 button onions, peeled
12 small cauliflower florets
12 baby corn cobs
4 tbsp salad oil
175ml/6floz chicken stock (see page 198)
salt and freshly ground white pepper
50ml/2floz white wine vinegar
2 handfuls curly endive
few sprigs of chervil, to garnish

Air-dried Wild Duck with a
Salad of Baby Vegetables (see
page 113)

ROAST TEAL WITH SMOKED HAM AND TURNIPS

4 PORTIONS
4 teal
8 savoy cabbage leaves
20 baby turnips
salt and freshly ground white
    pepper
2 tsp oil
50g/2oz unsalted butter
50g/2oz mirepoix (leek, celery,
    carrot, shallot)
120ml/4floz dry white wine
300ml/10floz duck or brown
    chicken stock (see page 199
    or 198)
½ garlic clove, roughly
    chopped
1 sprig of fresh thyme
1 tsp sugar
8 slices air-dried ham

Probably the best English air-dried ham comes from Richard Woodhall in Waberthwaite, Cumberland. It is well worth seeking him out, and not only for this recipe. Alternatively, use Parma ham or Bayonne ham. If baby turnips are not available, use the smallest ones possible and cut them into the shape of small turnips.

Method

Remove the legs from the teal and the wish bones, and chop off the ends of the carcasses. Roughly chop these along with the necks and save for making the sauce.

Strip the cabbage leaves of the central rib and wash the leaves well. Cook in boiling salted water until tender, then refresh and drain. Peel the turnips, retaining their natural shape and leaving about 1cm/½ inch of their green tops.

Lightly season the teal both inside and out. Heat the oil and 15g/½oz of the butter in a roasting tray. Sear the teal on all sides in the hot fat, browning lightly. Transfer to an oven heated to 240°C/475°F/gas 9 to roast for 8 minutes. Once cooked, transfer them to a warm place to rest for 10 minutes. Once rested, remove both breasts from each bird, cover and keep warm. Roughly chop the carcasses and return these along with the legs and other bones to the roasting tray and brown well. Add the mirepoix and brown this lightly. Tip off the fat, pour in the white wine and reduce over high heat until it has almost all gone. Pour in the stock, add the garlic and thyme along with any juices that have run from the breasts. Reduce, simmering slowly until only about 200ml/7floz remains. Strain the sauce through a fine strainer, pressing it well to extract all the flavour and juices. Keep warm.

To Serve

Place the turnips, sugar, a little salt and pepper, 25ml/1floz of water and 25g/1oz of the butter in a saucepan, cover with a tight fitting lid and cook until tender, about 10 minutes depending upon their size. Once cooked, increase the heat, remove the lid and allow the water to evaporate. Remove and keep warm. Return the breasts to the oven for 2 minutes to reheat. Heat the remaining butter in a frying pan and toss the cabbage leaves to warm through. Arrange 2 leaves on each plate to entirely cover the surface. Lay 2 slices of ham over the leaves on each plate. Place the plates under a very hot grill for a few seconds just to warm the ham through. Place 2 teal breasts on to the ham on each plate, scatter the turnips around and spoon the sauce over the teal and on to the cabbage leaves.

WILD DUCK WITH PEAR AND GINGER

Method

Remove the legs and the front part of the carcass from the ducks. Remove the wish bone and truss the birds (see pages 218–20). Skin the legs and roughly chop these along with the carcasses.

Peel the ginger and cut it into fine julienne. Place in a saucepan with the sugar, water and the juice of the lemon. Bring to the boil. Peel the pears, cut each one in half and remove the core. With the syrup barely simmering, add the pear halves and cover. Simmer very gently for 15–20 minutes until the pears are cooked. Allow them to go cold in the syrup.

Lightly season the birds both inside and out. Heat the oil and butter in a roasting pan and sear the ducks on all sides, browning them lightly. Place them on to one breast, transfer to an oven heated to 240°C/475°F/gas 9 and roast for 5 minutes. Turn on to the other breast and roast for a further 5 minutes. Turn on to their backs and roast for a final 5 minutes. Once cooked, remove them from the oven and allow to rest for 10 minutes. Remove the breasts from the birds, cover and keep warm. Roughly chop the carcasses. Brown the chopped carcasses and legs in the roasting pan. Once browned, pour off the fat. Add the red wine and reduce it until almost gone. Pour in the stock and simmer for 15 minutes. Drain the pears from the syrup and cut them into neat 1cm/½ inch dice. Strain the syrup and save the julienne of ginger. Strain the stock into a clean pan then return to the boil with 150ml/¼pt of the syrup. Reduce this until only about 200ml/7floz remains.

To Serve

Return the duck breasts to the oven for 2 minutes to reheat. Strain the sauce through a fine strainer or muslin on to the pears and the ginger. Keep warm. Slice each breast into 5 or 6 slices. Spoon a little of the sauce into the centre of each plate. Fan a duck breast on to the sauce then spoon the remaining sauce and pears on to the plates and partly over the duck.

4 PORTIONS

2 wild ducks
15g/½oz fresh root ginger
225g/8oz caster sugar
300ml/½pt water
½ lemon
2 Williams pears
salt and freshly ground white pepper
2 tsp oil
15g/½oz unsalted butter
120ml/4floz red wine
475ml/16floz duck or brown chicken stock (see page 199 or 198)

ROASTED WILD DUCK WITH JUNIPER AND SHALLOTS

4 PORTIONS
2 wild ducks
20 shallots
salt and freshly ground white
    pepper
2 tsp oil
15g/½oz unsalted butter
175ml/6floz red wine
50ml/2floz port
4 crushed juniper berries
350ml/12floz duck or brown
    chicken stock (see page 199
    or 198)

Method

Truss the ducks (see pages 218–20). Peel the shallots leaving them whole and with the root end intact. Lightly season the ducks. Heat the oil with the butter in a roasting pan and sear the birds over high heat on all sides, browning them lightly. Place the ducks on to their sides and cook in an oven heated to 240°C/475°F/gas 9 for 6 minutes. Turn on to the other side and continue roasting for a further 6 minutes. Remove the birds and the shallots from the pan and allow them to rest for 10 minutes in a warm place.

Once rested, remove the legs and breasts from each bird, cover and keep warm. Roughly chop the carcasses. Pour the fat from the roasting pan and place over high heat. Add the chopped bones and brown them lightly. Pour in the red wine and the port and add the juniper berries. Reduce until only about a quarter remains. Pour in the stock and continue reducing until only about 200ml/7floz remains.

To Serve

Return the ducks to the oven for about 1 minute to reheat.

Pour the sauce through a fine strainer or muslin. Spoon a little of the sauce into the centre of the plates. Remove the wing bones from the breasts and carve each breast into 6 slices across. Lay the slices in a semi-circle on the sauce in the centre of each plate. Prop a leg against each breast, arrange the shallots around the duck and pour over the remaining sauce.

WOODCOCK

French: *Bécasse* German: *Waldschnepfe* Italian: *Beccaccia*

Very little is actually known about this, the most attractive and delicate-looking of all European game birds. The woodcock is to be found all over Europe and North America and in places as far afield as China, Burma, Russia and the Canaries. With its beautiful large eyes, long slender beak and wonderful camouflaged plumage of reddy browns, black and grey, it is a most distinguished-looking bird. I find it almost impossible to tell male from female and young from old, and, having done some research on the woodcock for this book, it would seem that even the experts have some difficulty. One thing for certain though is the high esteem in which the woodcock is held. Not only in shooting circles as a most worthy and prized quarry, evidenced by the woodcock club (to become a member you must have shot two woodcock, one with each barrel without reloading), and the way the sportsman carries the pin feathers of shot birds in his hat, but also by the gourmet. The culinary virtues of the woodcock have been long known. Brillat-Savarin once wrote: 'The Woodcock is a very distinguished bird but few people know its charms. It is in its full glory when roasted before the eyes of the hunter, especially the hunter who shot it.'

Many people disagree with the way woodcock is traditionally prepared as it is said to demean a magnificent bird. Once cooked, its entrails minus the gizzard are removed and chopped with a few other ingredients and then served with the bird.

There are few moments more exciting than the appearance of a woodcock bursting from cover on a frosty December morning, snaking through the trees offering the guns only a fleeting chance of a shot, or the cooking and eating of the first of the winter woodcock. The woodcock is in season from the 1st of October to the 31st of January in England and Wales, and from the 1st of September to the 31st January in Scotland. I prefer woodcock during December and January when they seem to carry a little more fat on them once the weather has turned cold.

SALMIS OF WOODCOCK

Salmis is a classical dish which can be made from any type of game, pheasant, partridge, snipe, wild duck, etc, or even from some poultry such as duck or guinea fowl. It is often mistakenly made from leftovers, which is obviously not a true example of this magnificent dish. Do not skimp on the quality of the red wine, the better the wine the better the sauce will be.

4 PORTIONS

4 woodcocks

salt and freshly ground white pepper

2 tsp oil

40g/1½oz unsalted butter

85g/3oz mirepoix (carrot, celery, shallot, leek)

15g/½oz mushrooms, roughly chopped

25ml/1floz cognac

175ml/6floz good quality red wine

300ml/½pt game stock (see page 200)

4 turned button mushrooms

Method

If preparing yourself, pluck the woodcocks including the heads, singe them well (see page 214) and remove the eyes from each bird. Truss each bird by twisting its head around and, using its beak like a skewer, push it through its thighs to hold the bird in shape. Wrap the legs of each bird in foil to stop them burning then lightly season.

Heat the oil in a roasting pan with 15g/½oz of the butter. Brown the woodcock over high heat on all sides. Place them on to one leg and transfer them to an oven heated to 240°C/475°F/gas 9. Roast for 3 minutes, turn the birds on to their other legs then roast for a further 3 minutes. Finally turn the birds on to their backs and roast for a further 3 minutes, 9 minutes in all. Remove the birds from the oven and allow to rest for 10 minutes.

Remove the foil from the legs of the birds. Carefully remove the legs and the breasts from each bird, place these in a pan along with their heads and keep them warm and covered. Remove the intestines and discard the gizzards, and put the intestines to one side. Roughly chop the carcasses. Heat a little of the remaining butter in a saucepan, add the mirepoix and mushrooms and the carcasses and brown. Pour in the cognac, ignite then pour in the red wine. Reduce the wine by at least two-thirds. Pour in the stock and add the intestines to the sauce, bring to the boil and reduce until only about 200ml/7floz remains. Pour the sauce through a fine strainer, rubbing it through well to extract all of the goodness and flavour. Strain the sauce again.

To Serve

Return the sauce to the boil then gradually add the remaining butter, piece by piece, until the butter has melted. Pour the sauce over the woodcock. Warm the sauce and the woodcock in a bain-marie for about 5 minutes to finish cooking the woodcock. Arrange 2 legs and 2 breasts on to each plate and pour the sauce over and around. Cut each head into two and pierce each breast with one half. (For real lovers of woodcock, the head is the best part.) Garnish with the turned mushrooms.

WOODCOCK WITH FOIE GRAS AND TRUFFLES

This dish must be the ultimate in indulgence, not recommended as everyday fare.

Method

If preparing yourself, pluck the woodcocks including the heads, then singe (see page 214), and remove the eyes. Truss each bird with its beak by twisting its head around and using its bill as a skewer, pushing it through its thighs to hold the bird in shape. Lightly season each bird. Loosely tie the slices of back fat over the breasts, and wrap the legs in foil to stop them burning. Heat a roasting tray, add 15g/½oz of the unsalted butter, then quickly brown the woodcocks on all sides over high heat. Place them on to one leg and transfer them to an oven heated to 240°C/475°F/gas 9 to roast for 4 minutes. Turn the birds on to their other leg and roast for another 4 minutes. Finally, turn the birds on to their backs and roast for a further 4 minutes. Remove the birds from the roasting tray and allow to rest in a warm place for 10 minutes. Heat the clarified butter in a frying pan and fry the croûtons until golden brown.

Remove the fat and the foil from the birds, carefully cut off the legs and the breasts and keep them warm along with the heads. Remove the entrails and discard the gizzards. Chop these together with the truffle. Heat the remaining butter in a frying pan, add the chopped entrails and truffle and cook for a few seconds. Add the Madeira and reduce until almost gone. Spread this mixture on to the croûtons. Roughly chop the carcasses, return these to the roasting tray and lightly brown them. Pour in the red wine and reduce until almost gone. Pour in the stock and reduce until only about 120ml/4floz remains.

To Serve

Return the woodcock and the croûtons to the oven for 1 minute to reheat. Strain the sauce through a fine strainer or muslin. Return the sauce to the boil, remove it from the heat and gradually add the chilled foie gras butter to the sauce, shaking the pan continuously until it has all melted. Keep the sauce warm but not hot. Place a croûton in the centre of each plate. Lay 2 legs half on to each croûton, place 2 breasts over these. Pour the sauce over and around. Prop a head against the breasts on each plate and serve.

4 PORTIONS
4 woodcocks
salt and freshly ground white pepper
4 slices of pork back fat
20g/¾oz unsalted butter
25g/1oz clarified butter (see page 208)
4 oval croûtons of white bread, about 7.5cm/3 inches × 5cm/2 inches
25g/1oz black truffle, finely diced
25ml/1floz Madeira
85ml/3floz red wine
350ml/12floz game stock or brown chicken stock (see page 200 or 198)
85g/3oz foie gras butter, well chilled (see page 208)

Roast Woodcock

Roast Woodcock

*Roast woodcock is traditionally served complete with its head and its
entrails spread on a croûte. The head is cracked and the brains eaten.
Many people, not surprisingly, shudder, not only at the thought of
eating the brains, but also the thought of having the head served.
Check with your guests before including the head!*

4 PORTIONS
4 woodcocks
salt and freshly ground white
  pepper
4 slices of pork back fat
40g/1½oz unsalted butter
25g/1oz clarified butter (see
  page 208)
4 oval pieces of white bread,
  about 7.5×5cm/3×2 inches
25g/1oz foie gras
2 shallots, finely chopped
25ml/1floz cognac
175ml/6floz red wine
350ml/12floz brown chicken
  stock (see page 198)
4 sprigs of watercress

Method

If preparing yourself, pluck the woodcocks including the heads,
then singe (see page 214). Truss each bird by twisting its head
around and using its bill as a skewer, pushing it through its thighs to
hold the bird in shape. Remove the eyes. Lightly season each bird
then tie the slices of back fat loosely over the breasts. Wrap the legs
in foil to stop them burning. Heat half the butter in a roasting pan
and quickly brown the woodcocks on all sides over high heat. Place
on to one leg and roast in an oven heated to 240°C/475°F/gas 9 for 4
minutes. Turn the birds on to the other leg and roast for a further 4
minutes. Finally turn the birds on to their backs and roast for
another 4 minutes. Leave to rest in a warm place for 10 minutes.
Melt the clarified butter in a frying pan and fry the bread until
golden brown.

Remove the fat and the foil from the birds and carefully cut off
the legs and breasts. Keep them warm, along with the heads.
Remove the entrails and discard the gizzards. Chop these together
with the foie gras.

Melt the remaining butter in a frying pan and fry half the shallots
until soft. Add the chopped entrails and foie gras. Cook for a few
seconds then add the cognac and flame. Spread this mixture on to
the croûtes, keep warm.

Roughly chop the carcasses, and add to the roasting pan with the
remaining shallots. Brown them lightly. Pour in the red wine and
reduce until almost gone. Pour in the stock and reduce by half.

To Serve

Return the woodcocks and croûtes to the oven for about 1 minute to
reheat.

Pour the sauce through a fine strainer or muslin. Place a croûte
in the centre of each plate. Lay 2 legs half on to each croûte, place 2
breasts over these, and, if desired, prop a head against this. Pour
the sauce over and around. Garnish with a sprig of watercress.

Roast Woodcock on a Potato Cake with Kumquats

4 PORTIONS

4 woodcocks

salt and freshly ground white
    pepper

4 slices of pork back fat

350g/12oz large potatoes

40g/1½oz clarified butter (see
    page 208)

115g/4oz kumquats

2 tsp oil

15g/½oz butter

85ml/3floz brandy

50ml/2floz dry white wine

350ml/12floz brown chicken
    stock (see page 198)

sugar, to taste

Method

If preparing yourself, pluck the woodcocks including the heads, then singe them well (see page 214). Truss each woodcock by twisting its head and using its bill as a skewer, pushing it through its thighs to hold the bird in shape. Remove the eyes. Lightly season each bird then tie the slices of back fat loosely over the breasts. Peel the potatoes and cut the potato into very fine strips. Season the potato and mix with the clarified butter. Heat a frying pan and divide the potato into 4 equal piles in the pan. Form each one into 25×10 cm/10×4 in cakes. Fry gently until golden brown on both sides. Keep warm. Slice the kumquats very thinly.

Lightly season the woodcocks. Heat the oil with the butter in a roasting pan and sear the birds on all sides. Place each bird on to one leg then roast in an oven heated to 240°C/475°F/gas 9 for 4 minutes. Turn the birds on to the other leg and roast for a further 4 minutes. Finally turn the birds on to their backs and roast for another 4 minutes. Remove the birds and leave to rest for 10 minutes. Remove the legs and breasts and keep warm. Roughly chop the carcasses. Pour off the fat from the roasting pan and add the chopped bones. Brown lightly then add the sliced kumquats and the brandy. Flame the brandy then add the white wine and reduce until almost gone. Pour in the stock and reduce by almost half.

To Serve

Return the woodcock and potato cakes to the oven for about 2 minutes to reheat.

Pour the sauce through a fine strainer or muslin. Check the sauce: if it is a little too tart for your liking, add just a tiny pinch of sugar. Place a potato cake in the centre of each plate, cross a pair of legs on these and top the legs with a pair of breasts. Pour a trickle of sauce over each bird and then pour the remaining sauce around the potato cakes. You could, if you wish, save about a quarter of the sliced kumquats as a little garnish.

WOODCOCK WITH GIROLLES

Method

If preparing yourself, pluck the woodcocks including the heads, singe them well (see page 214) and remove the eyes from each bird. Truss each bird by twisting its head around and, using its beak like a skewer, push it through its thighs to hold the bird in shape. Wrap the legs of each bird in foil to stop them burning then lightly season.

Using a small sharp pointed knife, trim each girolle of any root and dirt but do not wash them. Peel the potatoes and cut into fine strips using either a mandolin or by hand. Season the potato and mix it with the clarified butter. Heat a frying pan, divide the potato into 4 equal piles in the pan and form each one into a 10cm × 5mm/4 × ¼ inch cake. Fry gently until golden brown on both sides. Remove from the pan and keep warm.

Heat the oil in a roasting pan with half the butter. Brown the woodcock over high heat on all sides. Place them on to one leg and transfer them to an oven heated to 240°C/475°/gas 9. Roast like this for 4 minutes. Turn the birds on to their other legs then roast for a further 4 minutes. Finally, turn the birds on to their backs and roast for a further 4 minutes, 12 minutes in all. Remove the birds from the oven and allow to rest for 10 minutes.

Remove the foil from the legs. Carefully remove the legs and the breasts from each bird and keep them warm and covered. Remove the intestines and discard the gizzards, and put the intestines to one side. Roughly chop the carcasses. Heat the remaining butter in a saucepan, add the mirepoix and the carcasses and brown these. Once browned, pour in the Madeira and the red wine. Reduce until almost gone. Pour in the stock and add the intestines to the sauce. Bring to the boil and reduce until only about 200ml/7floz remains. Pour the sauce through a fine strainer or muslin.

To Serve

Return the legs and breasts to the oven for about 1 minute to reheat.

Add the girolles to the sauce and allow to sit over very low heat for a minute to cook the mushrooms. Place a potato cake in the centre of each plate. Place two legs on top of each cake then arrange two breasts on top of the legs. Arrange the girolles in a circle around the potato, strain the sauce again through muslin or a fine strainer and pour over the birds and the girolles.

4 PORTIONS
4 woodcocks
salt and freshly ground white pepper
34 small girolles
350g/12oz large potatoes
40g/1½oz clarified butter (see page 208)
2 tsp oil
25g/1oz unsalted butter
50g/2oz mirepoix (celery, carrot, shallot)
25ml/1floz Madeira
120ml/4floz red wine
300ml/½pt brown chicken stock (see page 198)

WOOD PIGEON

French: *Pigeon, Pigeonneau* German *Taube* Italian *Piccione*

Most people probably give very little thought to the humble wood pigeon, seen by many simply as a rather dull looking grey bird to be found either in grey flocks around our most famous landmarks or ravaging the farmers' crops in spring. Its culinary uses too seem to be very underrated. Yes, it is true that the meat can be a little dry or even tough, but like anything else, it will only be so if it is overcooked.

Pigeon will mostly be found for sale during late winter, after the game season is over, or early spring. The reason for this, as any dedicated pigeon shooter will tell you, is that during bad weather, or shortly after, because of the scarcity of food, the pigeons will flock more so than in the summer months. With all the birds together in one area raiding the small amounts of feed available they are easier prey for the hunter. The pigeon shooter can be spotted laden with hides and decoys during the early spring just as the farmer has sown his spring wheat or barley, or that favourite of any gourmet pigeon, the pea. This is the time of year the pigeon loves, a winter of starvation over, and the kind farmer laying out food everywhere. The wily pigeon will not miss the chance of gorging himself. Pigeons will eat up to two and a half times their own body weight in crops every day – little wonder they are regarded as vermin. Consequently, there is no closed season for pigeons and they find themselves fair game seven days a week, fifty-two weeks a year. On closer inspection, the pigeon is not the drab bird first thought. On the contrary it has a subtle beauty of its own. Although its colouring is predominantly grey through to black on its tail, up close, apart from its white bands across the wings and underside of the tail, it also has two white patches either side of its neck. Above these patches it has lustrous purple and green display feathers. The breast plumage, although grey, has a definite pinky tinge to it, especially when seen flying overhead caught in the sun. The final area of colour comes from the pigeon's rather dull red legs.

Terrine of Wood Pigeon (see page 129)

The squab or pigeonneau is different again. This is a pigeon which is especially reared for consumption, a practice that has been pursued as far back as the early Egyptians, as well as in Britain, especially during the sixteenth and seventeenth centuries. Then for many years the French seemed to take over. Happily they are now being bred in this country again. As would be expected, they are much more succulent and tender than their wild cousins and also smaller because they are much younger, only 4–6 weeks old.

Salad of Wood Pigeon

4 PORTIONS

2 wood pigeons

65ml/2½floz red wine vinegar

50g/2oz finely diced vegetables (celeriac, carrot, turnip, red and yellow pepper)

1 shallot, finely chopped

salt and freshly ground white pepper

2 tsp oil

15g/½oz unsalted butter

85ml/3floz olive oil

2 handfuls mixed lettuce leaves (curly endive, corn salad, lollo rosso, raddichio, red oak leaf)

few fresh chervil leaves, to garnish

Method

Remove the legs from the pigeons and chop off the parson's nose end of the carcasses. Remove the wish bones and truss the birds (see pages 218–20). Bring the vinegar to the boil in a saucepan, add the diced vegetables and shallot, and return to the boil. As soon as it comes back to the boil, remove the pan from the heat and leave to go cold.

Lightly season the pigeons both inside and out. Heat the 2 teaspoons of oil in a roasting pan, add the butter and quickly sear the pigeons on all sides. Roast in an oven heated to 240°C/475°F/gas 9, first on one breast for 3 minutes, on the other breast for a further 3 minutes, then finally on their backs for 3 minutes. When cooked, transfer the birds to a warm place to rest for 10 minutes.

Whisk the olive oil (saving about 1 tablespoon for the salad) into the vinegar and vegetables, and season as necessary. Tear the salad leaves into small pieces, wash and drain well.

To Serve

Remove the breasts from each pigeon, then remove the skin and the wing bone. Carve each breast into as many very thin slices as is possible. Lightly season the salad leaves and toss them with the reserved olive oil. Carefully and neatly arrange these in neat piles at 12 o'clock on each plate. Fan out a sliced breast of pigeon on to the plates in front of the salad. Whisk the dressing and again spoon it over the sliced pigeon. Scatter the chervil leaves over the dressing.

TERRINE OF WOOD PIGEON

This delightful terrine, although time consuming, is actually quite easy to make. Using only the simplest of ingredients, as it does, it could easily be made using other types of game, such as teal. When serving I like to use the smallest of yellow cherry tomatoes with a few leaves from the heart of an oak leaf lettuce, and fresh chervil leaves, all of which are grown specially for me, giving a wonderful splash of autumn colours.

ABOUT 20 PORTIONS
12 wood pigeons
350g/12oz pork back fat
salt and freshly ground white pepper
150g/5oz parsley
1 egg, separated
85ml/3floz double cream
10 thin slices of pork back fat, weighing about 25g/1oz each

Method

Remove the breasts from each pigeon (see pages 216–17) and save their livers. Discard the legs and carcasses. Cut the breasts of 11 of the pigeons, all the livers and the 350g/12oz pork fat into 1cm/½ inch dice. Heat a frying pan and, when hot, quickly fry the pork fat in small quantities for a few seconds. Drain well, saving the fat that runs off. Season the diced meat and livers and again, in a very hot frying pan with a little of the saved fat, quickly sear the meat and livers. Drain well and leave to go cold.

Pick over the parsley and remove its stalks. Wash well, squeeze dry and finely chop. Roughly cut up the two remaining breasts and place them in a food processor with 1 teaspoon of salt and process until smooth. Add the egg white and continue blending until it starts to stiffen. Rub the mixture through a strainer into a bowl set over crushed ice. Gradually add the cream, mixing it in well. Mix in the egg yolk. Add the chopped parsley, diced meat and fat, mixing well until it is incorporated evenly. Test the mousse by placing a teaspoon of the mixture into boiling water. If it is too firm, add a little more cream and test again.

Line a 28cm/11 inch terrine mould with the slices of back fat, making sure there are no gaps and that you leave an overhang of about 9cm/3½ inches all the way round. Fill the terrine with the pigeon mixture, pressing it in well to exclude any pockets of air. Fold over the overhanging fat to totally enclose the mousse. Top with a sheet of foil then the lid of the terrine. Place the mould in a roasting pan half-filled with boiling water and cook in an oven heated to 190°C/375°F/gas 5 for about 1 hour. To test whether the terrine is cooked, push a skewer into its centre. Touch the skewer against your lips; the terrine is cooked when the centre is just warm. Remove the terrine from the oven and leave to go cold. Chill for at least 24 hours before eating.

Roast Breast of Wood Pigeon with Girolles and Foie Gras

4 PORTIONS

4 wood pigeons

4 slices of streaky bacon, rinds
removed

350g/12oz large potatoes

salt and freshly ground white
pepper

40g/1½oz clarified butter (see
page 208)

2 tsp oil

25g/1oz unsalted butter

16 girolles

2 artichoke bottoms, cooked
and cut into 16 wedges

120ml/4floz Madeira

350ml/12floz brown chicken
stock (see page 198)

4 slices of fresh foie gras, each
weighing about 40g/1½oz

sprigs of fresh dill, to garnish

Try halving the quantities of this recipe and serve it as a first course.

Method

Remove the legs and wish bones from the pigeons. Place a slice of bacon over the breasts of each pigeon and tie in place. Peel the potatoes, then cut into fine strips using a mandolin or by hand. Season the potato and mix it with the clarified butter. Divide the potato into four and make into cakes about 10cm/4 inches in diameter and 6mm/¼ inch deep. Fry gently until golden brown on both sides. Remove from the pan and keep warm.

Lightly season the insides of the pigeons. Heat the oil in a roasting pan then add half the butter. Quickly sear the pigeons in the hot fat. Place them on one breast and roast in an oven heated to 230°C/450°F/gas 8 for 3 minutes, turn on to the other breast and roast for a further 3 minutes. Turn on to their backs and cook for a final 3 minutes. Keep warm. Carefully wipe the girolles clean to remove any dirt and grit – do not wash.

Pour off the fat from the pan and add the remaining butter. Fry the girolles and artichokes over a gentle heat until the artichoke is lightly browned and the girolles cooked. Remove them from the pan. Pour off the fat and add the Madeira. Reduce by half over high heat and then add the stock. Reduce again by half. Pour the sauce through a fine strainer or muslin.

To Serve

Remove the breasts from the pigeons. Keep warm along with the girolles, artichokes and the potato cakes. Heat a dry frying pan until very hot. Lightly season the slices of foie gras and quickly fry for 10 seconds on each side. Place a potato cake in the centre of each plate and top each one with a slice of foie gras. Place 2 pigeon breasts on top of these and arrange the girolles and artichokes around the plates, alternating them. Spoon a little of the sauce over the pigeon breasts and pour the rest on to the plates. Finish the dish off with a few sprigs of dill scattered over the sauce.

Roast Breast of Pigeon with Girolles and Foie Gras

Breast of Wood Pigeon with a Salad of Curly Endive

4 PORTIONS

2 wood pigeons

1 tbsp oil

60g/2¼oz cold unsalted
    butter, diced

1 shallot, roughly chopped

½ stalk celery, roughly
    chopped

120ml/4floz dry white wine

175ml/6floz game or brown
    chicken stock (see page 200
    or 198)

1 sprig of thyme

4 large spinach leaves

40 flat parsley leaves

salt and freshly ground white
    pepper

225g/8oz puff pastry (see page
    210)

1 egg yolk beaten with 1 tbsp
    milk

175g/6oz curly endive

2 tbsp walnut or olive oil

dash of sherry vinegar

1 tomato, blanched, skinned,
    seeded and diced

Method

Remove the legs and breasts from the pigeons (see pages 216–17), then skin the breasts and remove the sinew from the fillets. Roughly chop the carcasses and the legs. Heat the oil in a frying pan and when hot add 10g/¼oz of the butter. Quickly sear the pigeon breasts in the hot fat. Remove from the pan and leave to go cold. Add the bones and legs to the fat and quickly brown them. Add the shallot and celery and lightly brown these as well. Drain off the fat and add the white wine. Reduce this by half over high heat then add the stock and thyme and simmer for 15 minutes. Strain the sauce through a fine strainer and reserve.

Lay the spinach leaves out flat, place 4 parsley leaves on to each, and then a pigeon breast in the centre. Season lightly. Wrap the spinach around each breast so that it is completely enclosed. Roll out the pastry to 3mm/⅛ inch thick, divide it into four, then carefully and neatly wrap each pigeon parcel in pastry. Brush the pastry with the egg yolk beaten with the milk and chill for 30 minutes.

To Serve

Place the pigeon parcels on a greased baking sheet and cook in an oven heated to 220°C/425°F/gas 7 for 10 minutes. Pick through the curly endive and break the leaves into small pieces. Wash, dry well and season lightly. Beat the walnut oil and vinegar together, pour over the leaves and toss. Place a large pastry cutter, about 12.5cm/5 inches in diameter, in the centre of each plate. Fill these with the curly endive, pressing it in well. Bring the sauce to the boil, reduce the heat to low and gradually add the remaining butter, piece by piece, until it has all melted. Strain the sauce through a fine strainer or muslin. Remove the pastry cutter and place a pigeon parcel in the centre of the endive. Pour the sauce on to the plates around the endive. Scatter the diced tomato and remaining parsley leaves on to the sauce.

WOOD PIGEON WITH CRAYFISH AND MORELS

Fresh morels are best for this dish, but if they are not available then use dried ones. If using dried, then remember that they need to be soaked in cold water for about 2 hours before they are required.

Method

Remove the legs from the pigeons and discard. Remove the wish bones and chop off the ends of the carcasses, discarding these also. Lightly season the birds both inside and out, then loosely tie the slices of fat or bacon over the breasts.

Remove the stalks from the morels and discard. Cut the caps into strips and rinse them quickly in cold water and drain. Heat the oil and the butter in a roasting tray and quickly sear the birds on all sides in the hot fat, browning them slightly. Place them on to one breast and transfer them to an oven heated to 240°C/475°F/gas 9 to roast for 3 minutes. Turn the birds on to their other breast and continue roasting for a further 3 minutes. Turn the birds on to their backs and roast for a final 3 minutes. Once cooked, allow the birds to rest for 10 minutes. Pour off the excess fat from the pan.

Remove the intestinal tract from the crayfish by pinching the middle section of the tail between your thumb and forefinger, then twist and pull. Over medium heat, add the celery, shallot and garlic to the tray and gently fry this without colouring until it starts to soften. Add the crayfish and fry for about 30 seconds. Pour in the cognac and ignite, add the stock, white wine and the thyme, cover and cook the crayfish for 3 minutes. Once cooked, remove them from the pan, drain and allow to cool. Once the crayfish have cooled enough to handle, remove the tail meat and return the shells to the stock. Reduce this until only about 85ml/3floz remains. Strain the stock through a strainer, pressing it well to extract all the flavour and juices, then strain the stock through muslin.

Once the pigeons are rested discard the fat, remove their breasts and skin them.

To Serve

Return the breasts to the oven for 2 minutes to reheat. Return the stock to the boil, pour in the cream and add the morels. Reduce the sauce until it just starts to thicken, add the crayfish tails and keep the sauce warm. Carve each pigeon breast into 4 or 5 slices lengthwise, and spoon a little of the sauce on to the middle of each plate. Arrange the slices of pigeon on to the sauce and spoon the remaining sauce over the sliced breasts.

---

4 PORTIONS
4 wood pigeons
salt and freshly ground white pepper
4 slices pork back fat or streaky bacon
6–8 large morels
2 tsp oil
15g/½oz unsalted butter
20 crayfish
½ stalk celery, roughly chopped
1 shallot, finely chopped
½ garlic clove, roughly chopped
50ml/2floz cognac
225ml/8floz chicken stock (see page 198)
50ml/2floz white wine
1 sprig of thyme
120ml/4floz double cream

Breast of Wood Pigeon in a Puff Pastry Case with Morels

BREAST OF WOOD PIGEON IN A PUFF PASTRY CASE WITH MORELS

Use either fresh or dried morels for this recipe. If using dried, they must be soaked in cold water for at least 2 hours before using, to bring them back to their original state. If morels are not available, then any other wild mushroom will suffice.

Method

Roll out the pastry to 6mm/¼ inch thick. Cut out four plain or fluted 7.5cm/3 inch circles. Place on a baking sheet and using the point of a small knife lightly score a criss-cross pattern on top. Brush with the egg yolk mixed with the milk. Chill for at least 30 minutes. Bake in an oven heated to 220°C/425°F/gas 7 for 10–12 minutes or until golden brown. Remove the stalks from the morels and discard. Rinse the caps quickly in cold water and drain.

Turn the oven up to 230°C/450°F/gas 8. Remove the legs from the pigeons and discard. Truss the pigeons (see pages 218–20) and tie the pork fat in place over the breasts. Heat the oil in a roasting pan, season the insides of the birds then sear in the hot oil. Lay them on one breast, roast in the oven for 3 minutes, turn them on to the other breast and cook for a further 3 minutes. Finally place them on their backs and roast for a final 4 minutes. Leave in a warm place. Pour off the fat from the pan and add the Madeira and stock. Reduce over high heat until it just starts to thicken.

To Serve

Remove the string and the fat from the pigeons. Carefully remove each breast from the carcasses. Remove the wing bones and the skin. Cut each breast into 5 slices lengthways. Any juices that run from the pigeons while resting or during cutting can be added to the sauce. Cut the pastry circles across into two. Return the sauce to the boil then strain it through a fine strainer or muslin on to the morels. Cover the sliced pigeons breasts with foil and return them to the oven along with the pastry case for a minute to reheat. Over a low heat, gradually whisk the butter in to the sauce, piece by piece, until it has melted. Place the base of each case just off centre on the plates and fan a pigeon breast on to each one. Spoon the sauce and the morels over the meat then place a lid on top. Finish with a sprig of dill or chervil.

4 PORTIONS
2 wood pigeons
275g/10oz puff pastry (see page 210)
1 egg yolk beaten with 1 tbsp milk
16–20 morels
2 thin slices of pork fat
2 tsp oil
salt and freshly ground white pepper
50ml/2floz Madeira
175ml/6floz game or veal stock (see page 200 or 201)
20g/¾oz cold unsalted butter, diced
4 sprigs of dill or chervil

Roast Wood Pigeon with Thyme

4 PORTIONS

4 wood pigeons

salt and freshly ground white
    pepper

4 slices of pork back fat or
    streaky bacon

2 tsp oil

35g/1¼oz unsalted butter

1 shallot, finely chopped

115g/4oz mushrooms, finely
    chopped

½ garlic clove, crushed

25ml/1floz Madeira

50g/2oz mirepoix (carrot,
    celery, leek, shallot)

150ml/5floz red wine

350ml/12floz game or brown
    chicken stock (see page 200
    or 198)

2 tsp of fresh thyme leaves
    (save the stalks to flavour
    the sauce)

25g/1oz clarified butter (see
    page 208)

4 round croûtons of white
    bread, about 6.5cm/2.5
    inches in diameter

Method

If the birds come unprepared, save the livers and cut them into small dice. Remove the legs of the pigeons, roughly chop them and save to one side for later. Remove the wish bones, chop off the ends of the carcasses and save these along with the legs. Lightly season each pigeon inside and out, then loosely tie the slices of fat or bacon over the breasts. Heat the oil and 15g/½oz of the butter in a roasting tray. Quickly sear the birds on all sides in the hot fat, browning them slightly. Place them on to one breast and transfer them to an oven heated to 240°C/475°F/gas 9 to roast for 3 minutes. Turn the birds on to their other breasts and return them to the oven for 3 minutes. Turn the birds on to their backs and return them to the oven for a further 3 minutes. Once cooked, remove the birds from the pan and allow to rest for 10 minutes in a warm place. Heat the clarified butter in a frying pan and fry the croûtons until golden brown. Remove and keep warm. Heat the remaining butter in a saucepan, add the chopped shallots and the livers and fry them for a few seconds. Add the mushrooms and the garlic, mix in well and then pour in the Madeira. Season the mixture and cook it slowly until the moisture has evaporated.

Once the birds are well rested, discard the fat covering, remove the breasts and skin them. Cover the breasts and keep warm. Roughly chop the carcasses, add these along with the other saved bones to the roasting tray and over high heat brown them evenly. Add the mirepoix and brown lightly. Tip off the fat, pour in the red wine and reduce until almost gone. Pour in the stock, add the thyme stalks and any juice that has run from the breasts and reduce this until only about 225ml/8floz remains.

To Serve

Spread the mushroom mixture on to the croûtons and return these along with the breasts to the oven for 2 minutes to reheat. Strain the sauce through a fine strainer or muslin on to the thyme leaves and keep warm. Place a croûton in the centre of each plate, top each one with 2 breasts, then spoon the sauce over the pigeon and on to the plates.

ROAST BREAST OF WOOD PIGEON WITH A PIGEON PARFAIT

Method

Remove the legs from the pigeons and discard. I don't think it's worth using the legs as they tend to be scrawny and tough. Season inside and out. Cut each slice of bacon into two. Place one half over each breast of 6 of the birds and tie them in place. Remove the stalks from the spinach leaves, wash the leaves well then blanch them in boiling salted water for a few seconds, refresh then drain. Using a little of the butter, lightly grease six 85ml/3floz oval moulds. Pat the spinach leaves dry and line each mould with them, allowing at least a 1cm/½ inch overhang all round. Roll out the puff pastry to 6mm/¼ inch thick. Using the back of a small knife, score a criss-cross pattern on top. Beat the egg yolk and milk together and brush over the pastry. Chill for at least 30 minutes.

Once the pastry has rested, cut out six 7.5cm/3 inch circles. Bake in an oven heated to 230°C/450°F/gas 8 for 10–12 minutes or until golden brown.

Skin and remove the breasts from the saved pigeon and dice the flesh. Process the pigeon meat in a food processor with the garlic, the saved livers, and a little salt and pepper until smooth. Add the eggs and 50ml/2floz of the port. When well mixed, gradually add the clarified butter, then the cream. Rub the parfait through a sieve. Spoon the parfait into the lined moulds and fold over the overhanging spinach. Cover each one with a sheet of buttered foil.

Heat the oil in a pan and, when hot, add the remaining butter. Roll the pigeons in the hot fat, lay them on to one breast and cook in the oven for 4 minutes. Turn the birds on to their other breasts and cook for a further 4 minutes. Turn the birds on to their backs and cook for a final 4 minutes. Keep warm.

Turn the oven down to 200°C/400°F/gas 6. Place the parfaits in a roasting pan half-filled with boiling water and cook in the oven for 8 minutes. Pour off the fat from the pigeon roasting pan and add the remaining port. Reduce by half over high heat. Add the stock and continue reducing until it starts to thicken.

To Serve

Remove the breasts from the pigeons and skin them. Cut the pastry circles across into two. Reheat the pastry and pigeons in the oven for about a minute. Place the bottom half of each case on the plates at 12 o'clock. Slice each breast into 5 across and slightly at an angle. Lay the breasts so there is one coming out of either side of each case. Turn out the parfaits and place them on the plates at 6 o'clock. Strain the sauce over the meat and the plates. Top each pastry with its own lid and serve.

6 PORTIONS

7 wood pigeons, with their livers

salt and freshly ground white pepper

6 slices of streaky bacon, rinds removed

6 spinach leaves

40g/1½oz butter

450g/1lb puff pastry (see page 210)

1 egg yolk beaten with 1 tbsp milk

1 garlic clove, chopped

2 eggs

225ml/8floz port

225g/8oz clarified butter (see page 208)

85ml/3floz double cream

2 tbsp oil

450ml/¾pt duck or veal stock (see page 199 or 201)

Sautéed Fillet of Hare with Apples and Blackberries (see page 141)

FURRED GAME

*In Britain, furred game is confined to very few types: venison,
hare and rabbit. I have also included in this section a few
recipes on wild boar, not because it is available in the wild in
this country, but because it is now being farmed, albeit in
limited numbers. In other parts of the world, various animals
like bear and buffalo are classed as game. Squirrels are also
used for food, more especially in North America than other
countries, but even in Britain the grey squirrel is a legitimate
quarry, although not many people would admit to having tried
it. Unfortunately, the rabbit and to some extent the hare are
classed, like pigeon, as vermin, and as such have no closed
season. The fact that it is vermin, and of course vulnerable to
myxomatosis, has caused the wild rabbit to fall from culinary
favour, with most people now probably turning to domesticated
rabbits. This is a real shame, for the wild rabbit has a far
superior flavour, is very cheap and greatly undervalued. The
hare in this country does not seem to be held in the same esteem
as it is in the rest of Europe. Venison is therefore probably the
most widely used of the four-footed game and is now being
farmed in ever increasing numbers.*

*When choosing venison, the meat should be a dark red with a
fine grain, and its fat should be white and firm. The ears of
rabbits should be quite soft and tear easily. If pre-prepared
then the flesh should be quite dry not sticky. Rabbit should be
hung for 2–3 days only, having first been paunched. Hares
need a little longer, about 4–5 days, and venison is at its best
between 7–12 days. They need to be hung in a cold, well-
ventilated area where the air can flow freely. Obviously,
if the weather is warm then they will not stand for as long.*

HARE

French: *Lièvre* German: *Hase* Italian: *Lepre*

The hare is to be found all over the British Isles, througout Europe, Asia, North and South America, Australia and New Zealand, although not always in as large numbers as the rabbit. At first sight most people would mistake a hare for a rabbit, but this mistake is normally rectified once it begins to move. The hare is considerably larger than a rabbit but the most notable factors are probably the length of the ears, tipped with black, and the long legs. The coat of the hare is a warm rich brown whereas the rabbit is much greyer. The underside of the hare is white and, unlike the rabbit, it has a black line on the top side of the tail.

Neither the brown hare, which lives on arable low land, or the mountain or blue hare, which, as its name suggests, lives only in mountainous regions, are governed by a closed season, but they are not allowed to be offered for sale from March to July inclusive. In Britain they have never been seen as an important quarry – exciting and exacting they may be, but they are rarely the sole reason for a day's shooting. Through the rest of Europe, however, they are much more highly sought after.

The meat of the hare also differs greatly from that of the rabbit. Rabbit flesh is pale, almost chicken like, but the meat of the hare is very dark and strongly flavoured, like that of venison. It is essential when buying hare that you choose a young one as the older ones do tend to be very tough and stringy. A young hare can be recognized by its slender paws with the claws invisible behind the fur. A very good test of age on a young hare is that its ears will tear easily. For preference, allow the hare to hang for 4–5 days as it is best eaten quite fresh, not high.

Sautéed Fillet of Hare with Apples and Blackberries

Method

Remove the fillets from the saddles and trim off the sinew. Set aside. Chop the bones. Heat half the oil in a roasting pan and add the bones. Place in an oven heated to 230°C/450°F/gas 8 until lightly browned. Add the vegetables, return to the oven until golden brown. Pour off the fat, add the red wine and reduce over high heat until almost gone. Add the stock and crushed peppercorns and simmer for 20 minutes. Strain the sauce through a fine sieve.

Lightly season the hare fillets. Heat the remaining oil in a frying pan, add half the butter and quickly sear the fillets in the hot fat on both sides. Reduce the heat and continue frying for 2 minutes each side. The fillets should still be quite pink. Remove them from the pan and keep warm. Pour off the fat. Peel the apple and using a melon baller or parisienne cutter scoop out as many balls as possible. Add the remaining butter to the pan, add the apple balls and sugar and fry until golden brown. Keep warm. Pour off the fat, and add the Calvados. Pour in the sauce and return to the boil.

To Serve

Return the hare fillets and the apple to the oven for about 1 minute to reheat.

Strain the sauce through a fine strainer or muslin on to the blackberries. Spoon the sauce and blackberries on to the plates. Carve each hare fillet into 5 slices lengthways and fan these on to the sauce. Scatter the apple balls over the hare and the sauce.

4 PORTIONS
2 saddles of hare
4 tsp oil
2 shallots, finely sliced
1 stalk celery, finely sliced
25g/1oz leek, finely sliced
120ml/4floz red wine
225ml/8floz game stock (see page 200)
6 white peppercorns, crushed
salt and freshly ground white pepper
15g/½oz unsalted butter
1 dessert apple
15g/½oz sugar
50ml/2floz Calvados or brandy
85g/3oz blackberries

Fillet of Hare Wrapped in Puff Pastry with Hazelnuts

4 PORTIONS
2 saddles of hare
salt and freshly ground white
    pepper
2 tsp oil
25g/1oz cold unsalted butter
115g/4oz whole hazelnuts
½ orange
50g/2oz fresh white
    breadcrumbs
1 egg
2 tbsp double cream
350g/12oz puff pastry (see page
    210)
1 egg yolk beaten with 1 tbsp
    milk
85ml/3floz red wine
25ml/1floz port
225ml/8floz poivrade sauce
    (see page 203)
1 tsp redcurrant jelly

PANCAKES
50g/2oz plain flour
a pinch of salt
1 egg
milk
2 tbsp oil

Method

Remove the fillets from the saddles and trim off the sinews. Season lightly. Heat the oil in a frying pan, add half the butter and quickly sear the fillets all over, browning lightly. Leave the meat to go cold. Make the pancakes by sifting the flour and salt into a bowl. Make a well in the centre and gradually beat in the egg and enough milk to make a fairly thin batter. Heat the oil in a frying pan and add about 2 tablespoons of batter. Fry on both sides. Make 4 pancakes in the same way. Leave to go cold.

Lightly toast the hazelnuts under a hot grill. Rub off the skins and grind in a blender. Peel the orange, reserve the peel and squeeze the juice. In a bowl, mix together the nuts, breadcrumbs, the whole egg, cream and orange juice. Lay the pancakes on the work surface and spread with the nut mixture. Place a hare fillet on each one and roll the pancake around the fillet.

Roll out the pastry to 3mm/⅛ inch thick and cut into four. Carefully wrap each hare parcel in the pastry, sealing the edges with the egg yolk and milk. Chill for at least 30 minutes. Brush each pastry parcel with the beaten egg and cook in an oven heated to 220°C/425°F/gas 7 for about 12 minutes or until golden brown. Keep warm.

To Serve

Place the red wine, orange peel and port in a saucepan, bring to the boil and reduce over high heat by half. Pour in the poivrade sauce and add the redcurrant jelly. Bring back to the boil and reduce until about 175ml/6floz remains. Gradually whisk in the remaining butter, piece by piece, until it has all melted. Strain the sauce through a fine strainer or muslin and keep warm. Carve each pastry parcel into 6 slices. Pour the sauce on to the plates and arrange the slices in a circle on the sauce.

FILLET OF HARE WITH TURNIPS

Method

Remove the fillets from the hares and trim off all the sinews. Discard the bones. Peel the turnips and cut them into 4cm×3mm/1½×⅛ inch batons. 'Turn' the baby turnips to retain their shapes, leaving about 2.5cm/1 inch of the green top on. Cook the baby turnips in boiling salted water until tender then refresh in cold water.

Season the fillets. Heat the oil in a frying pan, add 15g/½oz butter and sear the hare over high heat. Reduce the heat slightly and continue cooking for 2 minutes on each side. The fillets should be still quite pink in the centre. Remove and keep warm. Pour off the fat, place over high heat, add the red wine and reduce until almost gone. Add the stock and reduce until about 200ml/7floz remains.

To Serve

Place the turnip batons into a saucepan with the water, the remaining butter, sugar and a little salt and pepper. Cover and cook until tender. Reheat the baby turnips in boiling salted water. Reheat the hare in an oven heated to 220°C/425°F/gas 7 for 1 minute. Drain the turnip pieces and divide into neat piles on the plates, just off centre. Strain the sauce through muslin and pour it around the turnips. Slice each fillet into 5 slices lengthways and fan these, half on to the sauce and half on to the turnips. Garnish with baby turnips.

4 PORTIONS
2 saddles of hare
450g/1lb turnips
12 baby turnips
salt and freshly ground white pepper
2 tsp oil
40g/1½oz unsalted butter
120ml/4floz red wine
300ml/½pt game stock (see page 200)
50ml/2floz water
pinch of sugar

FILLET OF HARE WITH WILD MUSHROOMS

Method

Remove the fillets from the saddles and trim off the sinew. Season lightly. Scrape away any dirt or roots from the mushrooms and cut them into 4cm/1½ inch pieces. Heat the oil in a frying pan, add 15g/½oz of the butter then quickly sear the fillets on both sides. Reduce the heat and fry for a further 2 minutes each side. The fillets should still be quite pink. Remove and keep warm.

Pour off the fat, add the remaining butter, lightly season the mushrooms and fry for about 1 minute over high heat. Remove and keep warm. Add the red wine and Madeira and reduce over high heat by about two-thirds. Add the stock and jelly and reduce by half. Add the cream and reduce slightly. Strain through muslin.

To Serve

Reheat the hare and mushrooms in the oven for 1 minute. Divide the mushrooms between the plates and arrange in neat piles. Pour the sauce around the mushrooms. Carve each fillet into 5 thick slices across at a slight angle. Arrange these slices around the mushrooms.

4 PORTIONS
2 saddles of hare
salt and freshly ground white pepper
200g/7oz mixed wild mushrooms (girolles, morels, pleurots, shiitakes)
2 tsp oil
35g/1¼oz unsalted butter
50ml/2floz red wine
50ml/2floz Madeira
300ml/½pt game stock (see page 200)
1 tsp redcurrant jelly
50ml/2floz double cream

JUGGED HARE

4 PORTIONS
1 hare
1 onion, thinly sliced
600ml/1pt dry cider
3 garlic cloves, roughly
    chopped
1 bay leaf
1 sprig of thyme
1 sprig of parsley
1 tsp wine vinegar
1 tbsp oil
4 slices of bacon, rinds
    removed and cut into
    lardons
24 button onions, peeled
24 button mushrooms, stalks
    removed
50g/2oz seasoned flour
175ml/6floz port
175ml/6floz red wine
a little game stock if needed
    (see page 200)
salt and freshly ground white
    pepper

This must be one of the oldest known British game recipes – think of game and it immediately springs to mind. Called civet *in France, it probably takes its name from the deep stoneware jug in which it was originally cooked. The sauce is enriched and thickened by its blood and if liked a little redcurrant jelly could be added to the finished sauce to just slightly sweeten it.*

Method

Mix the onion, cider, garlic and herbs together to make a marinade. Skin the hare (see page 221), carefully remove the innards, reserving only the liver with the gall bladder removed, and the blood. Mix the blood with the vinegar (this will prevent it from curdling). Store in a cool place until needed. Divide the hare into joints (see pages 222–3). Place these in the marinade and leave for about 6 hours, turning occasionally.

Heat the oil in a frying pan and quickly fry the bacon until browned. Remove from the pan, add the onions and mushrooms and fry until browned. Remove them from the pan, draining well, and set to one side until needed. Drain the hare from the marinade and pat dry. Dust with the seasoned flour then quickly sear in the hot oil on all sides until golden brown. Place the hare in a deep ovenproof casserole. Pour in the port and wine, then add the marinade. If the hare pieces are not covered (this will depend upon the size of the pan) then add some stock. Bring to the boil, skim then cover with a tight fitting lid. Cook in an oven heated to 200°C/400°F/gas 6 for about 1 hour or until the hare is tender.

Once the hare is cooked, carefully transfer to a clean pan. Add the mushrooms, bacon and onions and strain over the sauce. Purée the hare liver with the blood and press through a fine strainer. Return the hare and sauce to the boil, and skim if necessary. Once the sauce is boiling, remove the pan from the heat. Gradually add 2 ladlefuls of sauce to the blood and liver mixture, whisking constantly. Gradually whisk this mixture in to the hare. Return the pan to very low heat for a few minutes to reheat and finish cooking the blood. On no account allow the sauce to boil once the blood has been added. Check for seasoning then serve.

Sautéed Fillet of Hare with Celeriac

Method

Using a sharp knife, carefully remove the fillets from the saddles, and trim off all the sinews. Peel the celeriac. Either cut 20 batons from the celeriac, or turn 20 pieces into small neat barrel shapes about 4×1cm/1½×½ inch. Set to one side and roughly chop the remaining celeriac. Pour about 5mm/¼ inch of water into a saucepan, add 15g/½oz of the butter and the lemon juice. Add the chopped celeriac, season lightly with a little salt and cover with a lid. Bring to the boil and simmer until soft – about 10 minutes. Drain the celeriac, place it in a food processor and process until smooth. Transfer to a clean pan and add the cream.

Heat the oil in a frying pan. Lightly season the hare fillets, then sear on both sides over high heat. Reduce the heat slightly and cook for about another 4 minutes. Once cooked the fillets should still be slightly pink in the centre. Remove from the pan and rest in a warm place. Tip the fat from the pan and pour in the red wine. Reduce until almost gone then pour in the game stock. Reduce until about 200ml/7floz remains.

To Serve

Melt the remaining butter in a clean frying pan. Add the 20 pieces of celeriac, toss them in the fat and sprinkle with the sugar. Fry, tossing them occasionally, until golden brown. Place the hare fillets in an oven heated to 220°C/425°F/gas 7 for about 2 minutes to reheat. Gently reheat the celeriac purée and check the seasoning. Spread the purée into a circle in the centre of each plate. Carve each hare fillet into about 5 slices lengthways and fan on to the celeriac purée. Pour the sauce through a fine strainer or muslin and pour it around the celeriac. Place 5 pieces of the glazed celeriac attractively around each plate and top each piece with a small sprig of chervil.

4 PORTIONS
2 saddles of hare
1 celeriac
40g/1½oz unsalted butter
juice of ½ lemon
salt and freshly ground white pepper
50ml/2floz double cream
2 tsp oil
120ml/4floz red wine
300ml/½pt game stock (see page 200)
1 tsp sugar
4 sprigs of fresh chervil

RABBIT

French: *Lapin* German: *Kaninchen* Italian: *Coniglio*

When I watched *Watership Down*, I mused afterwards that there would hardly ever again be a dry eye when a rabbit was spotted – except in a farmer's eye that is. I must admit that for some time I did find it difficult to bring the gun to my shoulder.

The rabbit is one of the few quarry, along with the pigeon, that has no closed season, as they are both classed as vermin. This is due to the extensive damage it causes to both agriculture and forestry as well as its propensity to breed at an amazing rate. This ability lasts all year round, although the main breeding season is from early spring through to the summer. It is believed that the female rabbit is capable of breeding by the time it is eight weeks old and within 12 hours of giving birth it will breed again.

Considering how all the odds seem to be stacked against the rabbit, it is just as well it is so virile or it would soon die out. Not only is it pursued by man both as a food source and in order to protect his crops, it is also prey for any number of other predators – foxes, cats, stoats, badgers, owls, crows, the list is endless. But by far its biggest enemy is myxomatosis. The first case of this terrible, nay, appalling disease was reported in 1953 in Kent, and by 1973 it was thought that the rabbit population in Britain had fallen to only five per cent of what it had been some 20 years earlier. A rabbit suffering in the latter stages of the disease has to be one of the saddest sights I have ever seen. Despite all this, however, the rabbit will probably be around for some considerable time to come.

The flesh of the rabbit is very similar in colour to that of chicken, although the meat of a wild rabbit is quite a lot darker than its domesticated brother. Once cooked, the meat is much firmer than that of chicken and can, if not cooked with care, be quite dry. Nowadays, most rabbit meat found for sale is that of the domestic rabbit and is quite different from its wild counterpart. Wild rabbit has a much stronger flavour than that of the domestic which does tend to be a little bland. The domestic rabbit also tends to be a little larger than the wild, by at least a third. The one big advantage of using reared rabbit is that you do not have the problem of the lead shot. Wild rabbits for the table are best shot with a rifle rather than with a shot gun as this minimizes bruising and, of course, saves you picking out the bits of lead.

Consommé of Wild Rabbit with Parsley and Baby Leeks

Method

Carefully remove the meat from the rabbit saddle, remove the meat from both thighs. Roughly chop the bones. Heat the oil in a frying pan and quickly brown the bones. Drain the bones from the fat, place in a saucepan, cover with the water and bring to the boil. Reduce the heat to a simmer and skim. Add the chopped vegetables along with the bay leaf, parsley, peppercorns and garlic. Simmer for 1½ hours. Strain the stock through a fine sieve and leave to go cold. This should give about 750ml/1¼ pt: if not, then make it up to this quantity with water.

To Clarify

Very finely chop the thigh meat and mix with the chopped vegetables, parsley and egg whites in a saucepan. Stir in the cold stock and bring to the boil. Just as it comes to the boil, reduce the heat so that it just simmers. Simmer for 45 minutes. Strain the consommé through muslin or a strainer. Check the seasoning and add salt if necessary. If there is a thin film of fat on the top of the consommé this can be removed by pulling a sheet of kitchen paper over the surface.

To Serve

Cook the baby leeks in boiling salted water for 1 minute, then refresh in iced water. Cut each leek across into four at a slight angle. Lightly season the rabbit fillets. Spoon a little consommé into a pan and poach the fillets for 4 minutes – they should still be slightly pink in the centre. Cut across into 8 slices at a slight angle. Reheat the consommé. Divide the slices of rabbit and baby leeks between soup plates. Ladle in the hot consommé, and scatter over the parsley leaves to garnish.

4 PORTIONS
1 wild rabbit, jointed (see pages 222–3)
2 tsp oil
1.2l/2pt water
50g/2oz leeks, finely chopped
1 stalk celery, finely chopped
50g/2oz carrots, finely chopped
1 tomato, finely chopped
½ small onion, finely chopped
1 bay leaf
25g/1oz parsley
½ tsp whole white peppercorns
1 garlic clove

CLARIFICATION
50g/2oz leeks, very finely chopped
½ stalk celery, very finely chopped
1 tomato, very finely chopped
15g/1oz parsley, very finely chopped
2 egg whites
salt

GARNISH
8 baby leeks, trimmed
few parsley leaves

Roast Rabbit with Basil

2 PORTIONS
1 rabbit
25g/1oz caul
2 medium carrots
50g/20oz unsalted butter
salt and freshly ground white
    pepper
175ml/6floz chicken stock (see
    page 198)
50g/2oz noodles (see page 209)
2 tsp oil
50ml/2floz dry white wine
1 shallot, finely chopped
85ml/3floz double cream
8 fresh basil leaves
¼ of a lemon
basil leaves or sprigs, to
    garnish

Method

Skin, clean and joint the rabbit (see pages 221–3). Wrap both legs and the saddle in the caul – this will prevent them from drying out. Discard the carcass and the front legs, or turn them into stock. Trim the carrots into 4 × 1 cm/1½ × ½ inch barrel shapes. Melt 10g/¼oz of the butter in a saucepan with a little salt and pepper and a tablespoon of the stock. Add the carrots, cover with a tight fitting lid and put to one side. Cook the noodles in lots of boiling salted water for 2–3 minutes, then refresh under cold running water.

Lightly season the legs and the saddle. Heat the oil with 15g/½oz of the butter in a roasting pan. Sear the legs and the saddle on all sides until lightly browned. Roast in an oven heated to 230°C/450°F/gas 8 for 10 minutes, turning once. Remove the saddle and keep it warm. Return the legs to the oven for a further 5 minutes. Once cooked, remove and keep warm. Pour off the fat from the pan, add the white wine and the chopped shallot. Reduce this until the wine has almost gone. Pour in the stock and reduce over high heat until only about 50ml/2floz remains. Pour in the cream and reduce until it just starts to thicken. Pour the sauce through a fine strainer.

To Serve

Bring the carrots to the boil and cook them quickly until cooked but still a little crisp. Tear the basil leaves finely. Add 10g/¼oz of the butter to the noodles, heat through and season lightly. Return the rabbit to the oven for about 1 minute to reheat. Return the sauce to the boil then gradually add the remaining butter, piece by piece, until all the butter has melted. Keep the sauce warm. Remove the meat from the saddle and cut each fillet into 5 slices. Arrange a pile of noodles on to each plate at 3 o'clock. Drain the carrots and arrange them into neat piles opposite the noodles. Add the basil to the sauce and a little of the lemon juice. Pour this on to the plates, place a leg at 12 o'clock then the slices opposite this. Garnish with a few leaves or a sprig of fresh basil.

NOTE:

If the rabbit has its kidneys, flash fry in the pan once the rabbit has been removed and serve in the centre of the dish.

Poached Wild Rabbit with Girolles

Method

Ideally, ask your butcher to skin and joint the rabbit for you into the two hind legs and the saddle. Make sure that if he is willing to do this for you that he also gives you back the rib cage and forelegs etc. as well. Alternatively, follow the instructions on pages 222–3. Trim the meat away from the drumstick part of the leg leaving the bone clean. Remove the bone from the thigh, roll the meat and tie it with string. Leave the saddle whole. Wipe the girolles clean and use a small knife to scrape away any stubborn dirt.

Lightly season the rabbit. Heat the oil in a pan, add the butter and once it starts to sizzle add the rabbit and quickly sear the meat. Remove it all from the pan. Add the shallot and garlic and gently fry for about 1 minute. Pour off the excess fat then add the Madeira and wine. Pour in the stock and bring to the boil. Turn the heat down until barely simmering, add the thyme and rabbit and cover. Simmer very gently – do not allow to boil. After 6–8 minutes remove the saddle, cover and keep warm. After a further 6–8 minutes remove the legs and keep warm with the saddle. If you add a spoon or two of stock it will prevent the meat from drying out. Strain the stock then reduce rapidly over a high heat until only about one-quarter remains.

To Serve

Carefully remove the meat from the saddle, remove the string from the thighs, cover the meat and place it in a hot oven for about 1 minute to reheat. Pour the cream into the reduced stock, return it to the boil and reduce slightly until it just starts to thicken. Reduce the heat to very low and add the girolles. Pour a little of the sauce on to each plate and place 2 drumsticks on top. Cut 3 slices from each thigh and place the slices on the plates so that they are running off the drumsticks. Carve each fillet into 3 slices lengthways and lay these fanned out next to the leg. Spoon the sauce and girolles over.

Note

If girolles are not available, try using small cèpes or even ordinary button mushrooms, although these will not be so colourful or flavourful.

2 PORTIONS
1 good sized wild rabbit
16 fresh girolles
salt and freshly ground white pepper
½ tbsp oil
10g/⅓oz unsalted butter
1 shallot, roughly chopped
½ garlic clove, roughly chopped
50ml/2floz Madeira
85ml/3floz dry white wine
300ml/½pt chicken stock (see page 198)
3–4 sprigs of fresh thyme
175ml/6floz double cream

Roast Rabbit on a Bed of Watercress with a Port Sauce

2 PORTIONS
1 wild rabbit, jointed (see
    pages 222–3)
25g/1oz caul
salt and freshly ground white
    pepper
2 tsp oil
25g/1oz unsalted butter
120ml/4floz port
225ml/8floz veal stock (see
    page 201)
150g/5oz watercress, stalks
    removed

Method

Cut the caul into 3 pieces – 2 for the rabbit legs and one for the saddle. Wrap the legs and saddle and season. Roughly chop the bones and the front legs. Heat the oil in a roasting pan and add half the butter. Quickly sear the legs, saddle and bones in the hot fat. Roast in an oven heated to 220°C/425°F/gas 7 for 12 minutes, turning once. Remove the saddle and keep warm. Return the legs to the oven and continue roasting for a further 10 minutes. Keep warm. Pour off the fat from the roasting pan, add the port to the bones and reduce by half over high heat. Add the stock and reduce by half again.

To Serve

Remove the caul from the legs and saddle. Carefully remove the meat from the saddle and return to the oven for about 1 minute to reheat, with the legs. Melt the remaining butter in a pan, add the watercress leaves and cook gently for 1–2 minutes. Season to taste. Drain and spoon a circle of watercress in the centre of each plate. Carve each fillet from the saddle into thin slices, across at a slight angle. Arrange these in a circle on top of the watercress. Place a leg on top of this. Strain the sauce through a fine strainer or muslin and pour around the watercress.

Roast Rabbit on a Bed of Watercress with a Port Sauce

Wild Rabbit Braised with Endive

2 PORTIONS
1 wild rabbit
25g/1oz caul
2 endives
salt and freshly ground white
    pepper
2 tsp oil
25g/1oz unsalted butter
½ small onion, roughly
    chopped
½ stalk celery, roughly
    chopped
50g/2oz white of leek, roughly
    chopped
50ml/2floz dry white wine
300ml/½pt brown chicken
    stock (see page 198)
½ garlic clove, crushed
1 sprig of fresh thyme
1 bay leaf
2 tsp snipped chives

Method

Skin, clean and joint the rabbit (see pages 221–3). Wrap both back legs and the saddle in the caul – this will prevent it from drying out. Roughly chop the carcass and the front legs. Remove the outer leaves and any discoloured leaves from the endives. Lightly season the rabbit. Heat the oil and half the butter in a roasting pan. Sear the rabbit in the hot fat on all sides allowing them to brown. Remove from the pan and add the chopped bones. Fry until browned, then add the vegetables and fry until lightly browned. Pour in the white wine, bring to the boil and reduce slightly. Pour in the stock and add the garlic, thyme and bay leaf. Place the rabbit pieces and the endives into the stock, cover and bring to the boil. Transfer the pan to an oven heated to 200°C/400°F/gas 6 and roast for 20 minutes. Remove the saddle and the endives, cover and keep warm. Return the legs to the oven for a further 15 minutes. Once cooked, remove the legs and keep them warm along with the saddle and the endives. Strain the stock and reduce over high heat until only about 150ml/ ¼pt remains.

To Serve

Remove the meat from the saddle and cut each endive into two lenthways. Return these along with the legs to the oven for 2 minutes to reheat. Place two halves of endive side by side and slightly fanned in the centre of each plate. Slice each fillet into about 5 slices and arrange these in a semi-circle over the root end of the endive. Prop a leg in the hollow of the semi-circle over the root end of the endive. Return the sauce to the boil, remove it from the heat and add the remaining butter, piece by piece, until the butter has melted. Strain the sauce through a fine strainer or muslin on to the chives. Spoon the sauce over the legs and on to the plates.

ROAST AND BRAISED RABBIT WITH MUSTARD AND THYME

Method

Skin, clean and joint the rabbit (see pages 221–3). Wrap both legs and the saddle in the caul fat – this will prevent it from drying out. Roughly chop the carcass and the front legs. Cut off the ends of the courgettes, discard the central core and cut the remainder into long thin strips about 3mm/⅛ inch wide, and put to one side.

Heat the oil with half the butter in a roasting pan. Lightly season the legs and the saddle, then sear on all sides in the hot fat, browning them lightly. Roast in an oven heated to 230°/450°F/gas 8 for 10 minutes, turning once. Remove from the pan and keep warm. Reduce the oven to 200°C/400°F/gas 6. Brown the chopped carcass over high heat. Add the vegetables and brown lightly. Pour in the white wine and reduce by half. As it reduces, stir in all of the caramelized juices from the bottom of the pan. Pour in the chicken stock and return to the boil. Once boiling, return the legs, cover and place in the oven for a further 15 minutes. Once the legs are cooked, remove them from the stock, cover and keep warm. Strain the stock from the bones and vegetables and reduce over high heat until only one-third remains.

To Serve

Return the legs and saddle to the oven for about 1 minute to reheat.

Stir the mustard into the sauce, pour in the cream and boil until it starts to thicken. Pour the sauce through a fine strainer on to the thyme leaves. Check the sauce for seasoning and add a few drops of lemon juice. Keep the sauce warm.

Melt the remaining butter in a frying pan, add the courgette strips and season them lightly. Gently fry over medium heat tossing them often to prevent browning. Once cooked, drain them of all fat. Carefully remove the meat from the saddles. Cut each meat fillet into about 5 long slices. Divide the courgettes into neat piles just off the centre of the plate towards 12 o'clock. Pour the sauce on to the plates around the courgettes. Arrange the slices of saddle to one side of the courgettes and a leg on the other side.

2 PORTIONS
1 wild rabbit
25g/1oz caul
175g/6oz courgettes
2 tsp oil
25g/1oz unsalted butter
salt and freshly ground white pepper
1 shallot, roughly chopped
½ stalk celery, roughly chopped
½ small garlic clove, roughly chopped
½ small carrot, roughly chopped
50ml/2floz dry white wine
175ml/6floz chicken stock (see page 198)
½ tsp Dijon mustard
50ml/2floz double cream
2 tsp fresh thyme leaves
juice of ¼ lemon

Venison

French: *Venaison, Cerf, Chevreuil* German: *Hirsch, Reh* Italian: *Cervo, Capriolo*

The term 'venison' is used to describe the flesh of all types of deer, of which there are six varieties in Britain alone. These are the red and the roe deer, which are both native to Great Britain, fallow, sika, muntjac, and the Chinese water deer. In America, elk, mousse, and reindeer are also classed as venison. The ones most likely and frequently found for sale under the banner of 'venison' are the red and roe deer, the majority until recently coming from Scotland. I say until recently because there has been a great upsurge in venison farming, not only in this country but worldwide. It would be true to say that although deer have been hunted both for sport and food since Saxon times, very few people if asked would actually have tried venison as a meat. The majority of venison culled or farmed in this country ends up on tables on the continent, especially German tables where it is highly sought after.

The closed seasons for venison vary greatly depending upon species, sex and region, but broadly speaking they are from March until the end of October for the does, and from May to the end of July for the bucks, except in Scotland where the closed season for does is from February to October and from October until June for the bucks. These are only guidelines, however, as the closed seasons are quite detailed for each individual species.

There are differing schools of thought as to which deer is the best for the table, the French preferring the roe (*chevreuil*) to the red for instance. Personally, I have no worthwhile opinion other than the younger they are the better. The deer is the largest of our game animals here in Britain, and because of its size, it is not bought whole but in cuts as with lamb or beef. The various cuts closely follow those of lamb – saddle, leg, shoulder, fillet, chops, neck, etc. When using venison, I tend to stick to the saddle. Apart from being the most expensive cut, it is also the best – it requires less cooking and marinating and is much more tender and succulent than other cuts. Good quality venison is easily recognized by

Rosettes of Venison Rolled with Herbs and Served with a Creamy Poivrade Sauce (see page 157)

its dark red, finely-grained meat, and when covered with fat, the fat should be white and very firm. Marinating venison is also a subject open to discussion, but this is something I do tend to do. To add to the discussion there are also many differing types of marinade (see pages 206–7). Young animals do not always need marinating when the flavour of the venison will be more delicate. Normally, venison should be hung for 7 to 12 days, depending on weather conditions. The older the beast the longer it will need to hang and marinate, and, consequently, the stronger the flavour.

ROAST LOIN OF VENISON WITH RED AND GREEN PEPPERCORNS

4 PORTIONS

550g/1¼lb venison from the loin

10–12 strips of pork fat, for larding

2 tsp oil

15g/½oz unsalted butter

salt and freshly ground white pepper

50ml/2floz cognac

200ml/7floz veal stock (see page 201)

1 tsp redcurrant jelly

120ml/4floz double cream

1 tsp pink peppercorns

1 tsp green peppercorns

4 sprigs of fresh chervil or dill

Method

Trim off all the fat and sinew from the venison. Using a larding needle, lard the loin with the strips of fat. Heat the oil with the butter in a roasting pan. Season the venison, then sear in the hot fat on all sides until lightly browned. Roast in an oven heated to 230°C/450°F/gas 8 for 15 minutes, turning occasionally. Once cooked the venison should still be quite pink inside. Remove it from the pan and keep warm.

Pour off the fat from the pan, pour in the cognac and ignite it. Pour in the veal stock and add the redcurrant jelly and reduce by just over half.

To Serve

Add any juices that have run from the venison during resting to the stock. Add the cream to the reduced stock, return it to the boil and add the peppercorns. Reduce this until it starts to thicken. Carve the loin of venison into 16 slices. Spoon a little of the sauce into the centre of each plate, and arrange 4 slices of venison overlapping each other on top. Spoon the remaining sauce and peppercorns partly over the venison slices and on to the plates. Finish the dish with a sprig of fresh chervil or dill.

Rosettes of Venison Rolled with Herbs and Served with a Creamy Poivrade Sauce

Method

Reserve 12 leaves of each herb and finely chop the remainder. Melt 25g/1oz of the butter in a saucepan and fry the shallot for a few seconds until it starts to soften. Add the mushrooms and cook for 2 minutes. Pour in the Madeira and add the chopped herbs and breadcrumbs. Season then leave to go cold.

Lay the slices of pork fat out flat, slightly overlapping to form a sheet large enough to wrap around the venison. Spread the fat with the mushroom mixture. Place the trimmed loin on this and roll the fat around to enclose it completely. Chill for 30 minutes. When chilled, tie the fat loosely in place with string, at 1cm/½ inch intervals. Cut the loin into 8 rosettes, each about 4cm/1½ inches thick. Season lightly.

Heat the oil in a frying pan, add the remaining butter and quickly sear the rosettes on both sides. Reduce the heat and cook gently for 4 minutes on each side. Keep warm. Pour off the fat from the pan, pour in the red wine and reduce over high heat until almost gone. Pour in the poivrade sauce and add the redcurrant jelly. Reduce by about one-third. Place the rosettes in an oven heated to 220°C/425°F/gas 7 for about 2 minutes to reheat. Pour in the cream, return to the boil and reduce slightly. Strain the sauce through a fine sieve or muslin.

To Serve

Pour a puddle of sauce into the centre of each plate. Place 2 rosettes on to the sauce and scatter the reserved herbs around the edge of the sauce. 'Turn' 8 small, firm button mushrooms. Melt the butter in a pan, add the lemon juice and cook the mushrooms for a few minutes. Place 1 on top of each rosette.

4 PORTIONS

675g/1½lb loin of venison, trimmed weight

25g/1oz mixed fresh herbs (tarragon, coriander, parsley, dill)

40g/1½oz unsalted butter

1 shallot, finely chopped

50g/2oz mushrooms, diced

25ml/1floz Madeira

25g/1oz fresh breadcrumbs

salt and freshly ground white pepper

115g/4oz pork back fat, thinly sliced

2 tsp oil

85ml/3floz red wine

225ml/8floz poivrade sauce (see page 203)

1 tsp redcurrant jelly

85ml/3floz double cream

GARNISH (OPTIONAL)

8 button mushrooms

15g/1½oz unsalted butter

juice of ½ lemon

Medallions of Venison with
Chestnuts (see page 160)

MEDALLIONS OF VENISON WITH CHESTNUTS

Method

4 PORTIONS

12 × 50g/2oz medallions of venison, cut from the loin

salt and freshly ground white pepper

2 tsp oil

25g/1oz unsalted butter

20 whole shelled chestnuts

120ml/4floz red wine

85ml/3floz port

350ml/12floz game stock (see page 200)

1 tbsp double cream

150g/5oz unsweetened canned chestnut purée

12 flat parsley leaves

Lightly season the medallions. Heat the oil in a frying pan and add half of the butter. When sizzling, add the medallions and quickly sear in the hot fat on all sides. Reduce the heat and cook gently for 4 minutes each side. Keep warm. Pour off the fat from the pan and add the remaining butter and the whole chestnuts. Toss these in the butter over high heat for 1 minute then transfer to a roasting pan. Roast in an oven heated to 220°C/425°F/gas 7 for 8 minutes, turning occasionally. Keep warm.

Pour off the fat from the roasting pan, add the red wine and reduce over high heat until almost gone. Add the port and stock, bring to the boil and reduce by almost half.

To Serve

Mix the cream with the chestnut purée in a bowl. Return the medallions and roast chestnuts to the oven for about 2 minutes to reheat. Place the bowl in a bain-marie place over gentle heat to warm through. Place 3 teaspoons of the chestnut purée on to each plate and top with 3 medallions. Strain the sauce through a fine strainer or muslin and pour over the medallions and plates. Arrange 5 chestnuts on each plate and top each medallion with a parsley leaf.

LOIN OF VENISON WITH BLACKBERRIES

Method

4 PORTIONS

550g/1¼lb loin of venison, in two equal pieces, trimmed weight

175g/6oz blackberries

salt and freshly ground white pepper

2 tsp oil

15g/½oz unsalted butter

175ml/6floz red wine

350ml/12floz game stock (see page 200)

few drops lemon juice

fresh chervil leaves, to garnish

Reserve 20 of the best blackberries and purée the remainder. Rub through a fine sieve to remove the seeds. Lightly season the venison. Heat the oil in a frying pan and add the butter. Quickly sear the venison on all sides, reduce the heat and cook gently for about 8–10 minutes. The venison should still be quite rare in the centre. Keep warm. Pour off the fat from the pan, add the red wine and reduce over high heat until almost gone. Add the stock and blackberry purée and reduce by just over half.

To Serve

Place the venison in an oven heated to 220°C425°F/gas 7 for about 2 minutes to reheat.

Check the sauce for seasoning and add a few drops of lemon juice. Strain the sauce through a fine strainer or muslin and pour it on to the plates. Carve each piece of venison into 10 slices and lay 5 slices on to the sauce on each plate. Place 5 of the reserved blackberries in a circle around the meat then scatter a few chervil leaves over the top.

MEDALLIONS OF VENISON WITH KUMQUATS AND WALNUTS

Method

Season each medallion with pepper, put in a bowl and add the rosemary, thyme and walnut oil. Leave to marinate for 12 hours.

Finely slice about 50g/2oz of the kumquats and set to one side. Cut the remaining kumquats into quarters. Put these in a saucepan with the water and sugar, bring to the boil and simmer for about 2 minutes. Leave to go cold.

Remove the medallions from the oil and allow the excess oil to run off. Lightly season both sides of each medallion with salt. Heat a frying pan and, when hot, add the butter. Quickly sear the medallions in the hot fat on both sides, then reduce the heat and fry gently for about 3 minutes each side. They should be slightly on the rare side. Keep warm. Pour off the fat from the pan, add the red wine and sliced kumquats, bring to the boil and reduce until almost gone. Pour in the stock and 2 teaspoons of the kumquat syrup, return to the boil and reduce by about half.

To Serve

Place the medallions in an oven heated to 220°C/425°F/gas 7 for about 1 minute to reheat.

Heat 2 teaspoons of the walnut oil from the marinade in a frying pan, add the quartered kumquats, strained of the cooking syrup, and the walnuts. Fry gently for 1 minute. Strain the sauce through a fine strainer or muslin. Drain the kumquats and walnuts from the oil and arrange them in piles in the centre of each plate. Pour the sauce around. Place 2 medallions on each plate next to the kumquats.

4 PORTIONS

8 × 85g/3oz medallions of
   venison, cut from the loin
freshly ground white pepper
1 sprig of fresh rosemary
1 sprig of fresh thyme
4 tbsp walnut oil
175g/6oz kumquats
50ml/2floz water
25g/1oz sugar
salt
15g/½oz unsalted butter
120ml/4floz red wine
300ml/½pt game stock (see
   page 200)
50g/2oz whole shelled walnuts

MEDALLIONS OF VENISON WITH A MOUSSE OF PEAS

4 PORTIONS

8 × 85g/3oz medallions of
    venison cut from the loin
sufficient cooked marinade to
    cover the medallions (see
    page 207)
900g/2lb fresh peas
salt and freshly ground white
    pepper
a little sugar
1 egg
1 egg white
25ml/1floz double cream
25g/1oz unsalted butter
2 tsp oil
150ml/¼pt red wine
350ml/12floz game stock (see
    page 200)

Method

Soak the medallions in the marinade for 12 hours before cooking. Shell the peas and cook them in boiling salted water with a little sugar until soft. Refresh and drain well. Save about 1 tbsp peas for garnish, then purée the remainder in a liquidizer along with the whole egg and the egg white until smooth. Pass the purée through a fine sieve then mix in the cream and a little seasoning if necessary. Using a little of the butter, butter 4 × 85ml/3floz round moulds. Spoon the pea mixture into the moulds and give each mould a few sharp taps on the work surface to expel any air. Cover each mould with buttered foil, then cook in a bain-marie in an oven heated to 200°C/400°F/gas 6 for 20 minutes.

While the mousses are cooking, drain the medallions from the marinade. Lightly season each medallion. Heat the oil and remaining butter in a frying pan, then seal the medallions on all sides. Reduce the heat slightly and cook for 3 minutes on each side. When cooked, they should still be slightly pink inside. Remove the medallions from the pan and keep warm. When the pea mousses are cooked, remove them from the oven and keep these warm also.

Pour off the fat from the pan and add the red wine and 120ml/4floz of the marinade. Reduce over high heat until it has almost gone. Pour in the game stock and reduce until only about 200ml/7floz remains.

To Serve

Return the medallions and the pea mousses to the oven for about 1 minute to reheat. Strain the sauce through a fine strainer or muslin. Tip the mousses from their moulds and place one on each plate just off centre. Spoon a little of the sauce on to the plates in front of the mousses. Place 2 medallions on each plate in front of the mousse, and spoon the remaining sauce over the medallions and on to the plates. Quickly reheat the reserved peas in a little boiling water then scatter these on to the sauce.

WILD BOAR

French: *Sanglier* German: *Wildschwein* Italian: *Cinghiale*

Sadly, the wild boar is not to be found in the British Isles any longer. It has been extinct since about the seventeenth century, but is still to be found wild throughout the rest of Europe where it is still a quarry species. Wild boar is now being farmed in Britain, albeit in limited numbers, but I'm sure it will soon become more widely available. In the wild state, wild boar is really only edible up to one year old, after that it becomes extremely tough. Up to six months old the boar is given the name 'marcassin', and from six months to one year it is known as 'bête rousse'. It receives many more different names as it grows older – it lives up to thirty years old – but as it is no longer edible I shall not list them. Because of its similarity to pork, any recipe that is suitable for pork will also be suitable for boar, but it is much stronger in flavour with a more pronounced gamey taste and it should always be marinated before using.

Cutlet of Wild Boar with a Salad of Red Cabbage

4 PORTIONS
4 cutlets of wild boar
150ml/¼pt cooked marinade
    (see page 207)
350g/12oz red cabbage
1 small onion
salt and freshly ground white
    pepper
2 tsp sugar
4 tbsp salad oil
4 tbsp walnut oil
5 tbsp sherry vinegar
2 tsp oil
15g/½oz unsalted butter
300ml/½pt veal stock (see page
    201)
1 tsp fresh thyme leaves

Method

The day before the dish is required, make up the marinade and marinate the cutlets in the refrigerator. Cut the red cabbage into quarters, remove the core and very finely shred the leaves. Peel and cut the onion into quarters and finely shred. Mix the cabbage and the onion together then season with salt, pepper and the sugar. Add the salad oil and walnut oil along with the vinegar and mix in well. Leave to stand for at least 24 hours.

Next day, drain the boar from the marinade, strain off 150ml/ ¼pt and keep it to one side for use in the sauce. Lightly season the cutlets. Heat the oil with the butter in a frying pan and fry the cutlets, searing them first then lowering the heat until cooked, about 10 minutes. Once cooked, remove from the pan and keep warm. Pour off the fat from the pan, add the marinade and reduce until it has almost gone. Pour in the veal stock and reduce until only about 175ml/6floz remains.

To Serve

Drain the cabbage from all its juice. Place the cutlets in an oven heated to 230°C/450°F/gas 8 for about 2 minutes to reheat. Bring the sauce back to the boil then pour it through a fine strainer or muslin on to the thyme leaves. Allow this to infuse for a couple of minutes and keep the sauce warm. Divide the cabbage salad into neat piles in the centre of the warmed plates. Pour the sauce around the cabbage and prop a cutlet half on and half off the cabbage.

Medallions of Wild Boar with Banana

An unusual combination I agree, but it does work!

Method

Trim off the fat and sinew from the four medallions. Make up the marinade and put the meat in. Leave overnight. When ready to cook, drain the medallions from the marinade, strain off 150ml/¼pt and keep it to one side for the sauce. Lightly season the medallions. Heat the oil and 15g/½oz of the butter in a frying pan and quickly fry the medallions on both sides, so the meat is slightly pink in the centre. Once cooked, remove them from the pan and keep warm. Pour off the fat, add the marinade and reduce until it has almost gone. Pour in the veal stock and reduce until only about 200ml/7floz remains. Pour the sauce through a fine strainer on to the mustard, stir well and keep warm.

Cut the bananas into 1cm/½ inch dice. Melt the remaining butter in a clean frying pan, add the diced banana and sprinkle with the sugar. Fry until golden brown.

To Serve

Place the medallions and banana in an oven heated to 230°C/450°F/gas 8 for about 2 minutes to reheat.

Divide the banana evenly and neatly arrange in the centre of the warmed plates. Place 2 medallions on top of each pile and pour the sauce around.

4 PORTIONS

8 × 65g/2½oz medallions of boar cut from the saddle

cooked marinade, sufficient to cover the medallions (see page 207)

salt and freshly ground white pepper

2 tsp oil

40g/1½oz unsalted butter

350ml/12floz veal stock (see page 201)

1 tsp grain mustard

3 bananas

2 tsp caster sugar

Creamy Scrambled Eggs with Kidneys in a Light Port Sauce (see page 169)

EGGS AND LIVERS

This section of the book is devoted to two items that are really by-products of poultry and game, but a work on the subject would be incomplete without them. Firstly eggs. Although I have described them as a by-product, I suppose they are not really that, especially chicken eggs, as a chicken kept for laying only goes on to become a boiling fowl. Eggs, of course, are a cornerstone of cookery and diet worldwide. Without them, the world would be a poorer place, despite the bad publicity they have had recently in Britain. I believe they are still a safe and versatile source of food and one which I have not stopped eating nor changed my ways of cooking them. Chicken eggs are not the only eggs to be considered. The eggs of all our game and poultry birds are edible, so why not try them? They all vary slightly from one to the other, not only in shape and size, but also in colour, flavour, and texture.

On the other hand, liver definitely is a by-product, with the exception of foie gras, where the meat of the bird is the by-product. Livers from all types of poultry and game are used. Of the furred game, venison liver is probably the best, with a powerful flavour and a texture similar to lambs' liver. Any recipe for lambs' liver would suit venison liver.

EGGS
French: *Oeufs* German: *Eier* Italian: *Uova*

Probably the most universal of all foods, the egg has been a staple of the world's diet since time began. Their versatility and nutritional value gives them a very important place in our eating habits. Chicken eggs, of course, are the most common and widely used, but the list of edible eggs truly stretches the imagination. Duck, goose, quail, guinea fowl, bantam, pheasant, turkey and gull are the most eaten next to chicken eggs, but we must not forget fish eggs. From sturgeon, we get the most expensive eggs of all – caviar – then salmon, lumpfish, cod and herring roes, they are all eggs.

The chicken egg, like the chicken, has suffered in quality and flavour thanks in the main to battery farming. The yolks vary in colour from pale yellow to dark orange. This depends upon the amount of yolk colourant – normally in the form of beta carotene in the commercial feeds – which is determined by the farmer deciding which shade of yellow is most likely to attract customers. Of course, we had the scare of salmonella poisoning from raw eggs, caused it would seem from the practice of turning the innards of the dead chicken into food for the living, not, I am sure you will agree, a very appetizing thought. If you buy free-range eggs as far as possible, then I believe you will not encounter this problem. The myth of a brown egg being better, both in flavour and quality, than a white one is exactly that, a myth. It is interesting to note that, whereas Europeans seem to prefer brown eggs and more especially speckled eggs, in America a white egg is favoured.

Duck eggs have always had a problem with salmonella poisoning. This is mainly because their shells are much thinner and porous than that of the chicken. To avoid this, don't buy dirty duck eggs or ones that appear to have been washed. They have a much higher fat content than hens' eggs, making them more difficult to digest – and also a larger yolk. Their shell colour can range from white to grey to pale blue.

Goose eggs tend to vary in size but generally are equivalent to three chicken eggs. The shells are white in the domestic varieties and are very strong in flavour. The yolk of water birds do tend to be richer in colour and flavour than those of land birds. Goose eggs have always been renowned for making exceptional cakes – and for scrambling.

The eggs of the quail are the smallest of the commercial eggs, although in relation to the size of the quail they are anything but small. They have pretty but brittle shells and a very thick membrane – for this reason they are much easier to peel while still warm. Their yolks are extremely large in proportion to the size of the egg and they are much more dense than chicken eggs, with the whites being a little waterier.

Guinea fowl eggs are very similar in size and texture to chicken eggs. Their pointed end is more pronounced, however, with the shell being chalk white and very smooth.

Pheasant eggs are a dirty grey brown colour with extremely tough shells. Use them like chicken eggs, although they are slightly smaller.

Gull eggs are probably the most expensive of all the birds' eggs – not surprising as they are not domesticated and gulls never nest in easily accessible places. They are always sold cooked. Their shells are olive brown and speckled dark brown, and their yolks are a very rich orange.

CREAMY SCRAMBLED EGGS WITH KIDNEYS IN A LIGHT PORT SAUCE

Method

Remove the core from the kidneys, cut into neat dice and season. Break the eggs into a bowl, season with a little fresh pepper and whisk well. Melt one-third of the butter in a small frying pan, and quickly brown the diced kidney until seared but still pink. Remove the kidneys from the pan and keep warm. Pour off the fat. Add the port and reduce over high heat by half. Add the stock and reduce until it just starts to thicken. Keep warm.

Melt 25g/1oz of the butter in a heavy-based pan over low heat. Add the eggs and cook, stirring continuously, until they start to thicken. Add the cream and a little salt. Once the eggs are ready, place a 10cm/4 inch diameter cutter in the centre of each plate. Spoon the scrambled eggs in, leaving a well in the centre of each ring. Gradually whisk the remaining butter into the sauce, piece by piece, until melted. Mix a little of the sauce with the kidneys and spoon into the wells in the eggs. Pour the remaining sauce on the plates around the scrambled eggs. Remove the rings and serve.

4 PORTIONS

10 eggs
3 lambs' kidneys
salt and freshly ground white
   pepper
50g/2oz cold unsalted butter,
   diced
175ml/6floz port
225ml/8floz veal stock (see
   page 201)
50ml/2floz double cream

TARTLET OF SCALLOPS AND SPINACH WITH POACHED DUCK EGGS

Duck eggs of course are not the only eggs you can use for this dish —
try ordinary chicken eggs or quail eggs.

4 PORTIONS
4 duck eggs
225g/8oz shortcrust pastry (see
   page 211)
225ml/8floz tomato sauce (see
   page 203)
3 tbsp vinegar
900ml/1½pt water
675g/1½lb fresh spinach
salt and freshly ground white
   pepper
4 cleaned scallops, white meat
   and coral diced
50g/2oz cold unsalted butter,
   diced
120ml/4floz double cream
1 tomato, blanched, skinned,
   seeded and diced
few tarragon leaves

Method

Roll out the pastry and use to line four 10cm/4 inch tart tins. Bake blind in an oven heated to 200°C/400°F/gas 6 for 10 minutes. Pour the tomato sauce into a pan and reduce by one-third. Remove from the heat. Poach the duck eggs in the vinegar and water for 3–4 minutes. Refresh in iced water. Remove the stalks from the spinach and wash the leves well, blanch these in boiling salted water then refresh in iced water. Drain and squeeze dry.

To Serve

Season the scallops. Melt 15g/½oz of the butter in a saucepan, add the scallops and fry gently for about 10 seconds. Add the spinach and stir it through well. Pour in the cream, bring to the boil and allow it to reduce slightly. Place the tartlet cases in the oven for 1 minute to reheat. Place the duck eggs into simmering water to heat through. Place the tomato sauce over gentle heat. Gradually whisk the remaining butter in to the tomato sauce, piece by piece, until all the butter has melted. Divide the spinach and scallops equally between the tartlet cases. Place a filled case in the centre of each plate. Drain the eggs, peel and place one in the centre of each tart. Pour the tomato sauce around the tart cases and spoon a little over the eggs. Scatter the tomato dice and the tarragon leaves on to the sauce.

SOFTBOILED EGGS FILLED WITH SMOKED SALMON

Not only does this make a good first course but a wonderful breakfast as well. Imagine starting the day with smoked salmon – go on spoil yourself! Try it with a little poached haddock or fresh prawns instead of the smoked salmon.

Method

Cut the smoked salmon into strips about 2cm/¾ inch long by 3mm/⅛ inch wide. Boil the eggs for 4 minutes. When cooked, cut off the tops as neatly as possible and scoop the eggs out of the shells into a bowl. Break up the egg using a fork until it is in pieces but not mashed. Add the cream and the strips of salmon. Season and return the mixture to the shells.

To Serve

Serve in egg cups accompanied with a little tossed green salad if you are serving it as a first course.

4 PORTIONS
4 small eggs (size 5 will be
    sufficient for a first course)
50g/2oz smoked salmon
2 tsp double cream
salt and freshly ground white
    pepper

SOFTBOILED QUAILS' EGGS IN A NEST OF FRENCH BEANS

Method

Top and tail the beans, then cook them in boiling salted water for 3 minutes. Refresh in iced water then drain. Softboil the quails' eggs in water and vinegar for 2½ minutes. Refresh in iced water and peel when cool. Cut the beans in half at a slight angle. Mix the yoghurt and cream together, season to taste with the lemon juice, salt, pepper and the sugar.

To Serve

Mix the beans with the oil and a little seasoning. Form a nest in the centre of each plate and arrange 5 eggs in each nest. At the last minute, finely chop the herbs and mix them into the yoghurt dressing. If necessary thin it down with a little water – it should be of a pouring consistency. Spoon a little of the dressing over the eggs then pour a ribbon of the dressing around the beans.

4 PORTIONS
20 quails' eggs
175g/6oz French beans
1 tbsp vinegar
85ml/3floz natural yoghurt
85ml/3floz double cream
juice of ½ lemon
salt and freshly ground white
    pepper
pinch of sugar
2 tbsp walnut oil
15g/½oz mixed fresh herbs
    (chervil, tarragon, chives,
    dill)

Tartlet of Quails' Eggs and Wild Mushrooms

4 PORTIONS

24 quails' eggs

225g/8oz wild mushrooms
(girolles, chanterelles,
pleurots, cèpes)

2 handfuls curly endive

15g/½oz unsalted butter

salt and freshly ground white
pepper

85ml/3floz Madeira

85ml/3floz veal stock (see page
201)

150ml/¼pt double cream

4 × 7.5cm/3 inch shortcrust
pastry cases

2 tbsp walnut oil

4 sprigs of chervil

Method

Softboil the quails' eggs for 2½ minutes, transfer then to iced water then peel them. Pick through the mushrooms, removing any roots and brushing off any dirt. Tear the curly endive into small pieces, wash and drain well. Heat the butter in a saucepan and, when sizzling, add the mushrooms. Season lightly and fry over high heat for about 1 minute. Remove the mushrooms from the pan and pour in the Madeira. Reduce over high heat by half. Add the stock and reduce by half. Pour in the cream and reduce until it thickens.

To Serve

Have ready a pan of boiling water in which to reheat the eggs. Put the pastry cases in a warm oven for 2 minutes to heat through. Place a case in the centre of each plate. Lightly season the endive and toss it with the oil. Arrange the leaves around each tartlet case. Return the sauce to the boil and add the mushrooms. Drop the eggs into the boiling water and remove the pan from the heat. Fill each case with the mushrooms, draining off a little of the sauce. Drain the eggs from the water and place 6 in each case. Pour the remaining sauce over the eggs and top with a sprig of chervil.

Puff Pastry Case Filled with Quails' Eggs and Vegetables

This quick and easy dish makes a wonderfully light, colourful first course. It would also be a good lunch main course dish – just increase the amount of eggs and add a few more vegetables.

Method

Blanch all the vegetables in slightly salted boiling water until cooked but still crisp. Refresh in iced water then drain. Poach the quails' eggs in water and the white wine vinegar so they are cooked but still with soft yolks. When cooked refresh them in iced water.

Roll out the pastry to 6mm/¼ inch thick. Using the back of a small knife, lightly score a criss-cross pattern on the top and brush with egg wash, and cut into 4 × 10cm/4 inch circles. Chill for at least 30 minutes. Once rested, bake in an oven heated to 220°C/425°F/gas 7 for 10–12 minutes or until golden brown. Keep warm.

Bring the stock and wine to the boil and reduce until only about one-quarter is left. Add the cream and return to the boil. Remove the pan from the heat and gradually whisk in the butter, piece by piece, until it has all melted. Add the vegetables and keep warm. Do not allow the sauce to boil.

To Serve

Place the poached eggs into a pan of hot but not boiling water to reheat for about 30 seconds. Cut each pastry case in half. Lay the bottom half of each case on the plates, drain the eggs from the water and divide between the cases. Spoon the sauce and vegetables over, top each one with a pastry lid and finish off with a sprig of fresh dill.

4 PORTIONS

24 quails' eggs

275g/10oz puff pastry (see page 210)

1 large courgette, diced

1 small red pepper, deseeded and diced

1 small yellow pepper, deseeded and diced

1 large carrot, diced

115g/4oz celeriac, diced

salt

1 tbsp white wine vinegar

1 egg yolk beaten with 1 tbsp milk

300ml/½pt chicken stock (see page 198)

50ml/2floz dry white wine

85ml/3floz double cream

115g/4oz cold unsalted butter, diced

4 sprigs of dill

Puff Pastry Case Filled with
Quails' Eggs and Vegetables
(see page 173)

WARM POACHED EGGS IN A TOMATO AND TARRAGON VINAIGRETTE

This dish is suitable either as a first course or a light lunch. If tarragon is not available, then try using basil or marjoram.

4 PORTIONS
4 eggs
4 tomatoes
50ml/2floz olive oil
25g/1oz shallots, roughly
    chopped
½ tbsp tomato purée
½ garlic clove, crushed
50ml/2floz tarragon vinegar
2 sprigs of fresh tarragon
50g/2oz unsalted butter, diced
salt and freshly ground white
    pepper
¼ head of curly endive

Method

Blanch and skin the tomatoes. Remove the seeds from 2 tomatoes, cut the flesh into neat dice and save this to garnish the finished dish. Roughly chop the remaining tomatoes along with the seeds of the first two. Heat the oil in a saucepan, add the shallots and cook gently until they soften. Add the tomatoes and stir in the tomato purée, followed by the garlic and half the tarragon vinegar. Save sufficient leaves from the fresh tarragon to sprinkle over the finished plates and reserve. Add the remainder, stalks as well, to the sauce. Bring to the boil and simmer over low heat for 10 minutes. When cooked, allow the sauce to cool then pass it through a strainer. Do not force it through – all you want is the resulting liquid. Poach the eggs in a shallow pan of water mixed with the remaining tarragon vinegar.

To Serve

Gently reheat the sauce over low heat then gradually whisk in the butter, piece by piece, until melted. Season and keep the sauce warm but do not allow it to boil. Wash the lettuce leaves, drain and dry well. Drain the eggs and place one egg in the centre of a warm plate. Scatter over the tomato dice and spoon the sauce over the eggs and on to the plates. Arrange a few curly endive leaves around the eggs then sprinkle with the reserved tarragon leaves.

LIVERS

French: *Foie* German: *Leber* Italian: *Fegato*

By far the most important of all the liver to come from any animal is duck or goose in the form of foie gras. Not any old duck or goose though. The best foie gras comes from France where they are specifically reared and fed to produce a swollen fatty liver acknowledged by gourmets the world over as a great delicacy, their meat being of secondary importance. Not only is it the most sought after of livers, but also extremely expensive – although worth every penny. Ordinary duck livers, like chicken livers, are, however, very cheap and form the basis for many great dishes. It's not only domesticated fowl though, that have edible livers. Far from it. The livers of all game may be used, be it pheasant or quail, venison or hare. The livers of most game birds are similar to those of domestic fowl and can be used in identical ways. Flavours will vary – pheasant liver is very like that of chicken, whereas grouse livers are darker, smaller and have a more pungent flavour, much like the meat of the bird. The same analogy can be made between the rabbit and venison. Apart from the obvious uses for liver, such as pâtés and salads, they can also be used to thicken certain sauces. When choosing livers, they should always be bright and firm – old livers look dull and lifeless.

SALAD OF CHICKEN LIVERS AND GIROLLES

Be careful to choose whole firm livers for this dish.

4 PORTIONS
24 chicken livers
24 small girolles
2 handfuls mixed salad leaves
 (corn salad, raddichio, red
 oak leaf, curly endive, etc.)
salt and freshly ground white
 pepper
2 tsp oil
25g/1oz unsalted butter
1 shallot, finely chopped
50ml/2floz sherry vinegar
25ml/1floz Madeira
250ml/9fl oz brown chicken
 stock (see page 198)
2 tbsp walnut oil

Method

Trim the chicken livers to remove any green gall bladder staining, sinew and fat. Using a small knife, trim off any root and scrape away any dirt from the girolles – do not wash them unless they are very dirty. Wash the salad leaves well, drain and dry.

Lightly season the chicken livers. Heat the oil in a frying pan and add half the butter. Quickly sear the livers until lightly browned. Cook for no more than 1 minute. Remove the livers from the pan and allow to cool. Add the shallot and vinegar and reduce until it has gone. Pour in the Madeira and the stock, and reduce until only about 175ml/6floz remains. Pour the sauce through a fine strainer into a clean pan.

To Serve

Toss the salad leaves with the walnut oil and a little salt and pepper. Arrange the leaves neatly in the centre of the plates. Return the sauce to the boil, then over very low heat add the girolles. Leave in the sauce for 1 minute, add the chicken livers and leave for a further minute. Drain the livers and girolles and arrange them alternately around the salad. Return the sauce to the boil and remove it from the heat. Gradually add the remaining butter, piece by piece, until it has melted. Strain the sauce through a fine strainer or muslin and pour it over the livers and girolles.

Mousse of Chicken Livers with Basil and Tomato

Method

Cut away the gall bladders and any green parts from the chicken livers. Place in a food processor with the garlic and a little salt and pepper, and process until smooth. Add the egg and process again until well mixed. Pour in the port then gradually add 150ml/¼pt of the cream. Strain the mixture through a fine sieve. Leave it in the refrigerator until needed.

Wash the spinach leaves well and remove the stalks. Blanch the leaves in boiling salted water for a few seconds then refresh in iced water. Lightly butter 4 round or oval 85ml/3floz moulds. Pat the spinach leaves, dry and line each mould with the leaves allowing an overhang all the way round. Spoon the liver mixture into the moulds, and fold the overhanging spinach over to enclose the mousse. Top each mould with a square of buttered foil. Place the moulds in a roasting pan half-filled with boiling water. Cook in an oven heated to 190°C/375°F/gas 5 for about 15 minutes. Keep warm.

To Serve

Bring the white wine to the boil in a saucepan and reduce over high heat until almost gone. Add the tomato sauce and the remaining cream and bring back to the boil. Reduce the heat to low and gradually whisk in the butter, piece by piece, until all the butter has melted. Shred the basil leaves and add them to the sauce. Keep warm. Carefully turn the mousses out of their moulds and place one in the centre of each plate. Spoon the sauce around. Place the diced tomato in neat piles on top of each mousse.

4 PORTIONS

115g/4oz chicken livers
½ garlic clove
salt and freshly ground white
    pepper
1 egg
50ml/2floz port
200ml/7floz double cream
4 large spinach leaves
50g/2oz cold unsalted butter,
    diced, plus extra for
    greasing
50ml/2floz dry white wine
50ml/2floz tomato sauce (see
    page 203)
12–14 fresh basil leaves
1 tomato, blanched, skinned,
    seeded and diced

CHICKEN LIVER PARFAIT

20 PORTIONS
250g/9oz fresh chicken livers
1 garlic clove, roughly
    chopped
2 tsp salt
400g/14oz unsalted butter
85ml/3floz port
25ml/1floz Madeira
3 eggs
120ml/4floz double cream
freshly ground white pepper
10 30×5cm/12×2inch slices of
    pork back fat
toasted brioche, to serve (see
    page 209)

Method

Trim the livers to remove any sinews and gall bladder staining. Place in a food processor with the garlic and salt. Melt the butter – it should be lukewarm, not hot. Process the livers until smooth, pour in the port and Madeira, then add the eggs. Gradually add the melted butter in a slow stream. Finally add the cream and pepper. Rub the mixture through a strainer into a bowl and chill.

Line an 28cm/11 inch terrine with the slices of fat, ensuring there are no gaps and leaving an overhang of at least 10cm/4 inches all the way round. Pour the parfait mixture into the terrine and carefully fold over the overhanging fat to totally enclose it. Cover the terrine with a sheet of foil then the lid.

To Cook

Heat a bain-marie of water, large enough to take the terrine, until almost boiling. Lay a few sheets of newspaper in the bottom and stand the terrine in this. Cook in an oven heated to 140°C/275°F/gas 1 for about 1½ hours. To test whether it is cooked, push a trussing needle into the centre and hold it for 10 seconds. When it is withdrawn it should be clean and barely warm in the centre.

Once cooked, remove the terrine from the bain-marie and allow to cool. Chill for at least 24 hours. To turn the parfait out, stand the terrine in warm water for a minute. Give it a couple of sharp taps on the work surface and it should slip out easily. Serve with slices of toasted brioche.

PITHIVIER OF CHICKEN LIVERS WITH A TOMATO AND LEEK BUTTER SAUCE

Method

Roll out the puff pastry to 3mm/⅛ inch thick. Cut out 4 × 11cm/ 4½ inch circles and 4 × 12.5cm/5 inch circles. Lay these on a floured baking sheet and leave to rest in the refrigerator. Heat 10g/ ⅓oz of the butter in a pan and when it starts to sizzle lightly fry the chopped shallots without colouring. Add the mushrooms, garlic and Madeira, season and slowly cook this until it has dried out. Remove from the heat and leave to go cold.

Remove the stalks from the spinach and wash the leaves well. Blanch in boiling salted water for a couple of seconds then refresh under cold water. Dry well. Remove any sinew and gall bladder staining from the livers, keeping them as whole as possible. Heat the oil in a frying pan, add 10g/⅓oz of the butter, then quickly sear the livers in the hot fat. Do not overcook them. Drain from the fat and leave to go cold.

To assemble the pithiviers, lay a spinach leaf over each of the smaller circles of pastry and place a spoonful of the mushroom mixture on to each leaf. Spoon the chicken livers on to this, season them lightly, then top with the remaining mushroom mixture. Fold the spinach leaves over completely enclosing the mushrooms and livers. Make sure there is a gap of 5mm/¼ inch between the edge of the pastry and the spinach all the way round. Egg wash the exposed pastry then lay the larger circle over the top. Press the edges down to form a seal and, using the back of a small knife, push the edges into a neat scallop shape. Using the point of a small knife, score curved lines on the top of each pithivier radiating out from the centre. Place on a greased baking sheet, brush with egg wash and chill for at least 30 minutes.

To Serve

Bake in an oven heated to 230°C/450°F/gas 8 for about 10–12 minutes or until golden brown. Bring the white wine to the boil and reduce until almost gone. Add the stock and reduce until only about 2 tablespoons remain. Add the leeks. Gradually whisk in the remaining butter, piece by piece, until it has all melted. At the last second, add the diced tomato, tear the basil leaves into small pieces and add to the sauce. Spoon the sauce on to the plates, place a pithivier in the centre of each and serve immediately.

Note

Try to use only whole livers: as long as the livers were only just sealed at the beginning they will still be pink when served. Duck livers will be equally as good if chicken livers are not available.

4 PORTIONS

175g/6oz chicken livers
350g/12oz puff pastry (see page 210)
100g/3½oz cold unsalted butter, diced
2 shallots, finely chopped
115g/4oz mushrooms, diced
1 garlic clove, crushed
25ml/1floz Madeira
salt and freshly ground white pepper
4 large spinach leaves
1 tsp oil
1 egg yolk beaten with 1 tbsp milk
120ml/4floz dry white wine
225ml/8floz chicken stock (see page 198)
85g/3oz leeks, diced
1 tomato, skinned, seeded and diced
8 basil leaves

Pithivier of Chicken Livers with a Tomato and Leek Butter Sauce (see page 181)

DUCK LIVER PARFAIT WITH A CRISP FILO PASTRY LID

For this dish I used 10cm/4 inch shallow moulds. If the moulds you use are deeper than 1cm/½ inch, the cooking time will be slightly longer.

6 PORTIONS
350g/12oz duck livers
salt and freshly ground white
  pepper
1 garlic clove
2 eggs
225g/8oz clarified butter (see
  page 208)
225ml/8floz port
85ml/3floz double cream
225g/8oz filo pastry (see page
  211)
melted butter for greasing
a little sea salt
350ml/12floz veal stock (see
  page 201)

Method

Carefully remove any gall bladders from the duck livers. Place in a good processor with salt, pepper and the garlic. Process until smooth, add the eggs and process again. Gradually add the clarified butter then 2 tablespoons of the port and the cream. Pour through a fine strainer.

To make the filo lids use the backs of the moulds you will be using to cook the parfaits. Brush the moulds with melted butter. Cut out 36 10cm/4inch circles from the filo pastry. Lay one on the upturned moulds and brush with melted butter. Cover each with 3 more circles, brushing each time with more melted butter. Place the last 2 circles on top and wrinkle them slightly to make a wavy edge, brushing with more butter. Sprinkle the tops with a little sea salt. Bake in an oven heated to 220°C/425°F/gas 7 for about 8–10 minutes. Remove from the moulds and keep warm.

Line each mould with buttered greaseproof paper then fill each one with the liver mixture. Place in a bain-marie and cook in the oven for 10 minutes or until set. While they are cooking, bring the remaining port to the boil and reduce by half. Add the stock and reduce until it starts to thicken.

To Serve

Strain the sauce through a fine strainer or muslin. Turn each parfait out on to the middle of the plate, pour the sauce around and place a lid on top.

Puff Pastry Case Filled with Duck Livers and Leeks

If baby leeks are not available then use normal leeks cut into thick batons.

Method

Roll out the puff pastry to a thickness of 5mm/¼ inch. Cut out 4 circles using either a plain or fluted 7.5cm/3 inch pastry cutter. Using the back of a small knife, score a criss-cross pattern on each circle of pastry. Allow the pastry to rest in the refrigerator for at least 30 minutes.

Trim the duck livers to remove any sinew, gall bladder and green staining, leaving them as whole as possible. Trim the leeks of their outer layers and green tops. Blanch in boiling salted water for 1 minute, then drain and refresh under cold water. Once cold, cut each leek into 5cm/2 inch pieces. Brush the pastry with the egg wash and cook in an oven heated to 220°C/425°F/gas 7 for 12 minutes or until golden brown. Transfer the cases to a wire rack to cool.

Lightly season the duck livers. Heat the oil in a frying pan with the butter and quickly fry the livers until cooked but still pink. Remove the livers from the pan and drain. Pour off the fat from the pan and add the port. Reduce by half over high heat. Pour in the veal stock and reduce by half.

To Serve

Cut each pastry case in two horizontally. Put them in the oven for a minute to reheat. Add the livers and the leeks to the sauce to warm through. Once warmed, place the bottom half of each case in the centre of serving plates. Drain the leeks and the livers from the sauce and arrange them attractively on the pastry. Pour the sauce through a fine strainer or muslin and pour it over the livers and leeks. Place a lid on top. If you have any fresh dill or chervil then finish each plate with a small sprig.

4 PORTIONS
225g/8oz duck livers
275g/10oz puff pastry (see page 210)
6 pencil-thin baby leeks
1 egg yolk beaten with 1 tbsp milk
salt and freshly ground white pepper
2 tsp oil
15g/½oz unsalted butter
175ml/6floz port
225ml/8floz veal stock (see page 201)
fresh dill or chervil (optional)

Ravioli of Duck Livers with a Sauce of Freshwater Crayfish

Be careful to choose whole duck livers for this dish.

10 PORTIONS
10 duck livers
85ml/3floz oil
100g/3½oz unsalted butter
salt and freshly ground white
    pepper
3 shallots, finely chopped
50g/2oz bacon, finely diced
25g/1oz mushrooms, finely
    chopped
½ garlic clove, crushed
350g/12oz ravioli paste (see
    page 209)
115g/4oz cooked spinach,
    chopped
1 egg, beaten
30 crayfish
600ml/1pt chicken stock (see
    page 198)
175ml/6floz dry white wine
5 tomatoes, blanched
20 fresh basil leaves
300ml/½pt double cream

Method

Trim the livers to remove any fat, sinew and green gall bladder staining, then cut each liver into 3 pieces. Heat 2 teaspoons of oil with 15g/½oz of the butter in a frying pan. Lightly season the livers then quickly sear them. Do not cook them, they only need to be seared. Remove from the pan and allow to cool. Add half of the shallots, the bacon, the mushrooms and the garlic and cook slowly until the mixture has dried out. Remove and allow to go cold.

To make the ravioli, divide the paste into two. Roll out both halves to a thickness of 2mm/½ inch either by hand or using a pasta rolling machine. If using a roller, you will have to roll it into strips about 7.5cm/3 inches wide: if rolling by hand then roll into two large squares. Mix the spinach with the mushroom mixture and check it for seasoning. Using two-thirds of the mushroom mixture, make 30 even piles on the paste, leaving a gap of about 2cm/¾ inch between each one. Place a piece of the duck liver on to each pile, then top with a little of the remaining mushroom mixture. Brush the egg between the piles of filling. Then cover with the other half of the paste. Press this top layer down well between the piles of filling to ensure a good seal. Cut the ravioli using a 5cm/2 inch round cutter.

To make the sauce, first remove the intestinal tract from the crayfish by pinching the middle section of the tail between your thumb and forefinger, then twist and pull. Bring the stock and the white wine to the boil, plunge in the crayfish and cook for 3 minutes. Remove the crayfish and allow them to cool. When cold, remove the meat from the tails and put to one side. Crush the heads and shells and add these to the stock and continue to boil, skimming as necessary, until only about 150ml/¼pt of the stock remains. Pour the stock through a strainer to remove the shells then pour it through muslin. Cut the blanched tomatoes into quarters, remove the seeds and cut the flesh into strips. Tear the basil into small pieces.

To Serve

Bring about 7l/12pt salted water to the boil. Pour in the remaining oil. Plunge in the ravioli and boil for 3–4 minutes. Remove and drain on a cloth. Return the stock to the boil, add the cream and the remaining shallots and reduce this slightly. Add the crayfish tails and the remaining butter, piece by piece, until all the butter has melted. Remove the pan from the heat and add the tomato strips and basil. Spoon a little of the sauce into warmed soup plates, place 3 ravioli in each plate then spoon over the remaining sauce.

Sautéed Foie Gras on a Bed of White Radish

The white radish complements the richness of the foie gras perfectly. If white radish is not available then try it with celeriac instead.

Method

Peel the radish and cut into fine strips either with a mandolin or by hand. Place in a bowl and season lightly with salt and pepper. Add the oil and vinegar and mix well. Check for taste and add the sugar if necessary. Leave to stand in the refrigerator for at least 24 hours.

To Serve

Reduce the vinegar in a saucepan over high heat until almost gone. Add the stock, Madeira and the orange peel and reduce this by just over half. Season the foie gras. Heat a dry frying pan and, when hot, fry the slices of foie gras quickly for about 30 seconds each side. Arrange the radish in the centre of the plates like a flat cake. Place a slice of foie gras on the top. Strain the sauce through a fine strainer or muslin and pour around the radish. Top each slice of foie gras with a sprig of chervil to add a splash of colour.

4 PORTIONS

4 slices of fresh foie gras, each weighing 50g/2oz
1 white radish, weighing about 275–350g/10–12oz
salt and freshly ground white pepper
2 tbsp oil
2 tbsp sherry vinegar
pinch of sugar
few sprigs of chervil, to garnish

SAUCE

50ml/2floz sherry vinegar
300ml/½pt veal stock (see page 201)
50ml/2floz Madeira
2 strips orange peel

Turbot with Foie Gras and Truffle Cream Sauce

This is bursting with cholesterol, but what a way to go!

Method

Skin the fillets of turbot, trim off any dark meat from the underside and discard. Butter an ovenproof pan, place the fillets in it, season, and add the fish stock and the sherry. Cover with buttered paper or foil and poach in an oven heated to 200°C/400°F/gas 6 for 4–6 minutes. When cooked, remove the fish from the pan, cover and keep warm. Turn the oven up to 220°C/425°F/gas 7.

For the sauce, reduce the liquor by at least two-thirds over a high heat. Add the cream and reduce until it starts to thicken.

To Serve

Lay the slices of foie gras on top of the fillets and place in the oven for about 30 seconds or until the foie gras goes soft. Add the truffle to the sauce, place a fillet on each plate and pour the sauce over and around. Serve immediately.

4 PORTIONS

4 × 175g/6oz fillets of turbot
10g/¼oz unsalted butter
salt and freshly ground white pepper
175ml/6floz fish stock (see page 199)
85ml/3floz dry sherry
225ml/8floz double cream
4 × 25g/1oz thin slices of foie gras
10g/¼oz diced truffle

STEAMED FOIE GRAS WITH A PURÉE OF FRESH PEAS

Although this is a very simple dish, the combination of flavours is superb. The foie gras needs to be cooked at the very last second as it cannot be reheated, and therefore it is essential to be well organized and to work quickly.

4 PORTIONS

4 × 65g/2½oz slices of fresh foie gras

450g/1lb fresh peas

salt and freshly ground white pepper

4 large spinach leaves

25ml/1floz sherry vinegar

85ml/3floz veal stock (see page 201)

40ml/1½floz double cream

20g/¾oz unsalted butter

Method

Shell the peas, cook in boiling salted water until soft then refresh in iced water. Drain well, purée and rub through a fine sieve. Remove the stalks from the spinach, blanch in boiling salted water and refresh in iced water. Lightly season the slices of foie gras then wrap each one in a spinach leaf. In a saucepan, reduce the vinegar until gone, pour in the veal stock and reduce it slightly.

To Serve

Add the cream to the pea purée and reheat gently. Check the purée for seasoning. Place the slices of foie gras into a steamer for 30 seconds. Spoon the purée in a neat circle in the centre of each plate. Return the sauce to the boil then gradually add the butter, piece by piece, until all the butter has melted. Carefully lift the foie gras from the steamer and place one slice on top of the purée on each plate. Pour the sauce around and serve immediately.

SALAD OF FOIE GRAS AND YOUNG SPINACH

4 PORTIONS

12 × 25g/1oz slices of fresh foie gras

1 egg, hardboiled

⅓ tsp Dijon mustard

25ml/1floz sherry vinegar

salt and freshly ground white pepper

65ml/2½floz salad oil

1 tbsp water

85g/3oz bacon

115g/4oz small young spinach leaves

Method

Remove the egg yolk and discard the white. Push the yolk through a fine sieve. Add the mustard, the vinegar and a little salt and pepper. Whisk in the salad oil then the water and check the seasoning. Cut the bacon into lardons and blanch in boiling water for a few seconds to remove the excess salt. Drain, then fry until crisp. Set to one side. Pick through the spinach leaves and remove any stalks, then wash and drain the leaves well.

To Serve

Put the spinach leaves into a bowl along with the lardons, lightly season and add the dressing. Toss well. Arrange the salad attractively on the plates. Lightly season each slice of foie gras. Heat a dry frying pan until very hot, and fry the foie gras, a few slices at a time, for about 10 seconds each side. Pour off any fat between batches. Arrange three slices on to each salad and serve immediately.

Parfait of Foie Gras

Whenever I have served this dish its accompaniment would be four small garnishes: kumquat marmalade, marinated white radish, a small leaf salad, and sliced cherry tomatoes with a basic dressing, and, of course, brioche. Try serving it with a Sauternes jelly, a salad of baby leeks or French beans.

10–12 PORTIONS
1 whole foie gras, weighing about 550g/1¼lb
900ml/1½pt strong chicken stock (see page 198)
85ml/3floz Madeira
salt and freshly ground white pepper
85g/3oz clarified butter (see page 208)
25g/1oz truffle (optional)

Method

Using a small sharp knife, carefully remove any green gall bladder staining from the liver. Cut the large lobe into three and the small lobe into two. Bring the chicken stock and Madeira to the boil in a saucepan. Remove it from the heat. Season the pieces of foie gras well, then plunge them into the hot stock. Allow them to sit in the stock until they are just soft. Remove them and allow to cool. Reduce the stock over high heat until only about 50ml/2floz remains. Rub the foie gras through a fine strainer into a bowl set over iced water. Pour in the reduced chicken stock. Warm the clarified butter to no more than blood heat, then add it to the chicken stock, stir well and leave the mixture to set, stirring occasionally. Finely chop the truffle and, when the mixture is almost set, gently fold it in. Transfer the parfait to a suitable-sized container and chill in the refrigerator until completely set.

To Serve

Turn the parfait out of its container gently. This is done by dipping the base of the container into hot water for a few seconds. Give it a sharp tap and it should just slip out. Cut the parfait into 1cm/½ inch slices. Serve it with warm brioche (see page 209).

SAUTÉ OF FOIE GRAS WITH ROASTED SHALLOTS

4 PORTIONS

4 slices of fresh foie gras, each
    weighing 50g/2oz

3 potatoes, each weighing
    115g/4oz

salt and freshly ground white
    pepper

40g/1½oz clarified butter (see
    page 208)

1 tsp oil

10g/¼oz unsalted butter

16 shallots, peeled

50ml/2floz sherry vinegar

50ml/2floz Madeira

300ml/½pt veal stock (see page
    201)

chervil, to garnish

Method

Peel the potatoes and cut them into fine strips, using either a mandolin or by hand. Place in a bowl and season lightly. Add the clarified butter and mix well. Divide the strips into four equal piles and form each one into cakes about 10cm/4 inches in diameter and 5mm/¼ inch deep. Heat the oil in the frying pan and gently fry the cakes until golden brown on both sides. Remove them from the pan and keep warm.

Heat the oil in a roasting pan, add the butter then the shallots. Season lightly then roast in an oven heated to 220°C/425°F/gas 7 for about 8–10 minutes, turning them occasionally. They should be nicely browned but still slightly crisp. Remove from the pan and keep warm. Pour off the fat. Place the pan over high heat, add the vinegar and reduce until it has almost gone. Add the Madeira and stock and reduce by half. Strain the sauce through a fine strainer or muslin.

To Serve

Season the slices of foie gras. Heat a dry frying pan and when hot quickly fry the foie gras for 30–40 seconds each side. Place a potato cake in the centre of each plate and lay a slice of foie gras on top. Place 4 shallots around each cake and pour the sauce on to the plates. To add a little colour to the finished dish, place a few leaves of chervil on top of each shallot.

Sauté of Foie Gras with Roasted Shallots

Terrine of Vegetables with a Centre of Fresh Foie Gras

20 PORTIONS

1 × 450g/1lb fresh foie gras

salt and freshly ground white
  pepper

1 tsp cognac

1 tsp port

1 tsp Madeira

175g/6oz carrots

115g/4oz turnips

115g/4oz celeriac

115g/4oz courgettes

50g/2oz French beans

275g/10oz calabrese

275g/10oz fresh girolles

25g/1oz unsalted butter

12–16 large spinach leaves

200g/7oz chicken breast,
  skinned and boned

2 egg whites

225ml/8floz double cream

25ml/1floz dry vermouth

tomato vinaigrette (see page
  205)

whole poached girolles, to
  garnish

Method

Leave the foie gras at room temperature until it becomes pliable. Using a small sharp knife, remove any gall bladder staining then the network of veins and nerves that run through the liver. Place the foie gras on to a sheet of cling film. Season the liver with salt and a few turns of white pepper. Mix the cognac, port and Madeira together and sprinkle over the liver. Roll the foie gras into a neat tight sausage shape then chill for at least 2 hours. The roll should fit snuggly inside the terrine mould.

Peel the carrots, turnips and celeriac, and cut into 6mm/¼ inch dice, keeping them all separate. Cut the courgettes and beans into similar sized dice. Break the calabrese into small florets, cutting off all the stalk. Blanch all the vegetables in boiling salted water for about 30 seconds, with the exception of the courgettes which should only be blanched for 10 seconds. Plunge into iced water to cool quickly. Cut off any root from the girolles, brush off any dirt and cut into 1cm/½ inch dice.

Melt 15g/½oz of the butter in a frying pan and quickly fry the girolles for about 10 seconds. Drain and cool. Pick off the stalks from the spinach leaves, wash and blanch in boiling salted water. Refresh under cold water.

Roughly chop the chicken, place in a food processor with 1 teaspoon of salt and process until smooth. Add the egg whites and process until they are well incorporated and the mixture stiffens. Rub the mixture through a fine strainer into a bowl set over ice. Gradually add the cream, mixing in well each time, then add the vermouth.

Drain the vegetables and pat them dry. Lightly butter a 28cm/ 11 inch terrine with the remaining butter. Line with the spinach leaves, allowing an overhang of at least 10cm/4 inches all the way around. Mix the vegetables and girolles with the chicken mousse. Put half of the vegetable mixture into the terrine, pressing it in well to exclude any air. Remove the cling film from the foie gras. Place the foie gras down the centre of the terrine then add the remaining vegetable mixture, again pressing it in well to ensure there are no air pockets. Fold the overhanging spinach over to totally enclose the mousse. Top with a sheet of buttered foil then the lid.

To Cook

Cook the terrine in a bain-marie in an oven heated to 190°C/375°F/ gas 5 for 50 minutes. To test whether the terrine is cooked, push a trussing needle into the centre of the terrine and hold it for 10 seconds. When removed, the centre of the needle should be just warm. Allow the terrine to cool then transfer it to the refrigerator for 24 hours. To turn the terrine out, stand it in warm water for about 30 seconds, give the terrine a couple of sharp taps on the work surface and it should then just slip out. Cut the terrine into 1cm/½ inch slices and serve with tomato vinaigrette, garnished with a few whole poached girolles.

SAUTÉED FOIE GRAS WITH TURNIPS

Method

Peel the larger turnips and cut into pieces the size and shape of cloves of garlic. 'Turn' the baby turnips to retain their natural shape, leaving about 2.5cm/1 inch of the green top on. Cook the baby turnips in boiling salted water until tender then refresh in cold water.

Bring the vinegar to the boil in a saucepan and reduce it until almost gone. Pour in the stock and reduce by about a quarter. Pour the sauce through a fine strainer or muslin and keep warm.

Place the pieces of turnips into a saucepan with the butter, water, sugar and a little salt and pepper. Cover the pan with a tight fitting lid and cook the turnips over moderate heat until tender.

To Serve

Heat a dry frying pan until very hot, lightly season the slices of foie gras and fry them for 15 seconds each side. Remove from the pan and keep warm. Reheat the baby turnips in a little boiling salted water. Divide the buttered turnips between the plates, pour the sauce around. Place a slice of foie gras on top of the turnips and garnish with the baby turnips.

4 PORTIONS
4 × 65g/2½oz slices of fresh foie gras
450g/1lb turnips
12 baby turnips
85ml/3floz sherry vinegar
225ml/8floz veal stock (see page 201)
25g/1oz unsalted butter
85ml/3floz water
½ tsp sugar
salt and freshly ground white pepper

Terrine of Foie Gras (see page 196)

Terrine of Foie Gras

4 PORTIONS
2 × 675g/1½lb duck livers
25ml/1floz port
25ml/1floz brandy
25ml/1floz Madeira
pinch of allspice
1½ tsp salt
1 tsp caster sugar
freshly ground white pepper

Terrine of foie gras has got to be one of the finest foods available to man. Served with slices of toasted homemade brioche, it is the most luxurious item I know. Not a recipe for the faint-hearted, however, as its price is quite forbidding, but no work on poultry could ever be complete without it. So here it is. Be brave – the reward is spectacular.

Method

If the livers seem a little firm, either soak them for a while in lukewarm water, or leave them at room temperature until they become pliable. Using a sharp knife, carefully cut away any gall bladder staining, then peel away as much of the thin membrane as possible. Remove the nerves and veins that run through the lobes. This is a very fiddly job and needs to be done with care and precision. You will have to cut quite deep in order to seek out all of these 'strings' but do try to keep the livers as whole as possible.

Mix all the remaining ingredients together in a large bowl. Add the livers and gently turn them around so that everything is evenly distributed. Cover with cling film and leave to marinate for 6 hours.

Lay a large lobe, with its outer surface downwards, into a 23cm/9inch terrine and press it in lightly. Top with the smaller lobes, again pressing lightly. Finish off the terrine with a large lobe, this time with its outer side uppermost. The terrine should be slightly overfull. Cover with the lid and place the terrine in a bain-marie of water warmed to no more than 70°C/158°F, with a few sheets of newspaper in the bottom. Cook in an oven heated to 110°C/225°F/gas ¼ for about 1½ hours. To test whether or not the terrine is cooked, push a trussing needle into the centre. Hold it for 10 seconds. When removed the centre of the needle should be barely warm. Allow to cool.

Have ready a wooden board just large enough to fit snuggly inside the terrine. After the terrine has cooled for about 1 hour, place the board on to the terrine, pressing lightly. Pour off the excess fat and reserve. Place a 700g/1½lb weight on top of the board and chill for 6 hours. Remove the weight and the board and pour over the reserved fat. Chill for at least 24 hours before serving.

STOCKS, SAUCES AND BASIC RECIPES

This section concentrates on the basic stocks required to go towards making a first class dish, as well as a few basic recipes and accompaniments. Without a good stock as its base, a sauce will only be a sauce, but with a well prepared and tended stock a sauce can become the highlight of the dish. In the professional kitchen the sauce chef is generally regarded as the most important member of the brigade, able to make or break a good meal more than anyone else. I am a great believer in making a sauce from a basic stock made from the bones of the meat with which it is to be served. Whether it be pheasant, duck or rabbit, always use the bones as far as is possible to make the sauce. Never discard a bone, save it in the freezer until you have enough, and make the stock from your store. Also keep the finished stock in the freezer, in small batches, ready to use.

To make a first class stock, and consequently a first class sauce, takes practice, time and patience. It can not be hurried, but above all it needs prime ingredients – you only get out what you put in. The hours spent simmering, skimming, and reducing a good stock pay off in the end with a sauce that is silky smooth, shiny and clear with an intense flavour. It is very rare for me to season a finished sauce: if the base stock is good and the main ingredients are seasoned before or during cooking then, unless you prefer highly seasoned food, this is normally enough.

Once made, the finished sauce should be served as soon as possible. If, however, you find that you must make a sauce a little in advance, then store it in a bain-marie or water bath over very low heat and cover it to prevent a skin from forming.

CHICKEN STOCK

2.75g/6lb chicken bones, wings
   and carcasses
900g/2lb white of leek
2 onions
4 stalks celery
2 garlic cloves
water to cover the bones
300ml/½pt dry white wine
2 sprigs of parsley
2 sprigs of thyme
1 bay leaf
1 tsp white peppercorns,
   crushed

All stocks are really very easy to make. Most people, however, seem not to bother. This chicken stock will keep for about 4 days in the refrigerator, or alternatively freeze it in small containers. This way you only need to remove sufficient each time for the particular dish and the rest stays fresh. If you have a few mushrooms or fennel, add these to the stock as well. Once the stock is made, try turning it into a glace. Reduce it down over a high heat until only about 300ml/½pt remains – this will now be extremely strong and it can be added in small quantities to a sauce that may be slightly lacking in flavour. In this form it will also keep about twice as long.

Method

Finely chop all the vegetables and garlic and wash them well. Remove any excess fat from the chicken bones and then rinse the bones in cold water. Place the bones in a saucepan, cover with fresh water and bring to the boil. As it comes to the boil, skim from time to time. Once boiling, reduce the heat so that it only just simmers and skim again. Pour in the wine and add the vegetables, herbs and peppercorns. Simmer for about 2 hours, skimming as necessary. Pour the stock through muslin.

BROWN CHICKEN STOCK

2.75kg/6lb chicken bones,
   wings and carcasses
450g/1lb leeks
1 onion
4 stalks celery
2 carrots
2 garlic gloves
85ml/3floz oil
1 tbsp tomato purée
water to cover the bones
1 sprig of rosemary
2 sprigs of thyme
1 bay leaf
1 tsp black peppercorns,
   crushed

Brown chicken stock has many different uses, as a base for a consommé, instead of veal stock, and of course in dishes that call for a brown chicken stock. As with white chicken stock this too will keep well in the refrigerator for about 4 days, or in the freezer. The flavour of the stock will change depending on how well the bones and the vegetables are browned initially. Overbrowning will result in a very bitter aftertaste which will get worse as the stock reduces.

Method

Finely chop all the vegetables and garlic and wash them well. Remove any excess fat from the chicken bones. Heat the oil in a roasting pan, add the chicken bones and turn them in the oil. Place in an oven heated to 230°C/450°F/gas 8 until they start to brown. Add the chopped vegetables, stirring them through well, then return the pan to the oven and continue browning. Once the vegetables and bones are a golden brown, dot with the tomato purée and return to the oven for a further 5 minutes. Transfer all the bones and vegetables to a saucepan. Deglaze the pan with about 300ml/½pt of water, scraping up all the caramelized juices from the pan. Pour this over the bones, cover with more water and bring to the boil. As it comes to the boil, skim it from time to time. Once boiling, reduce the heat so that it only just simmers. Skim again then add the herbs and peppercorns. Simmer this for about 1 hour, skimming as necessary. Pour the stock through muslin.

Duck Stock

As with all stocks this will keep either in the refrigerator for up to 4 days, or several weeks in the freezer. Use for any duck dish. By substituting water for the veal stock, it can be used as the base for a consommé as well. It is vitally important to make sure all the skin and fat is removed from the bones: if not, the result will be extremely fatty.

Method
Remove any excess fat and skin from the duck bones. Finely chop all the vegetables and garlic. Heat the oil in a roasting pan and add the bones. Turn in the oil and roast in an oven heated to 230°C/450°F/gas 8 or until they start to brown.

Stir in the chopped vegetables then return to the oven until the vegetables and bones are golden brown. Transfer everything to a saucepan. Deglaze the roasting pan with the red wine, scraping up all the caramelized juices. Pour over the bones, add the water and veal stock and bring to the boil, skimming from time to time. Once boiling, reduce the heat so that it only just simmers. Skim again, then add the herbs and peppercorns. Simmer for about 1½ hours, skimming as necessary. Strain the stock through muslin.

MAKES ABOUT 1.2L/2PT
1.75kg/4lb duck bones, wings and carcasses
1 onion
85g/3oz carrots
115g/4oz leeks
2 tomatoes
2 garlic cloves
2 tsp oil
225ml/8floz red wine
1.7l/3pt water
600ml/1pt veal stock (see page 201)
1 bay leaf
1 sprig of thyme
½ tsp black peppercorns, crushed

Fish Stock

The best bones to use for fish stock are those from turbot, brill, Dover sole, whiting and most white flesh fish. However, I do not normally use the bones of cod or haddock as I find they leave the stock with a dirty appearance. The stock will keep very well in a refrigerator for up to 7 days or can be frozen down into usable amounts.

Method
Remove any blood from the bones and, if using the heads, then remove the gills. Briefly soak the bones in cold water. Heat the butter in a heavy-based pan, add the vegetables and sweat for a few minutes. Add the white wine, reduce slightly, and then add the lemon juice and sufficient water to just cover the bones. Bring to the boil and skim frequently. When no more scum comes to the surface, after about 4–5 minutes, add the bouquet garni and simmer for 20–25 minutes. When ready, strain the stock through muslin.

MAKES ABOUT 1L/1¾PT
450g/1lb fish bones and trimmings
900g/2lb white vegetables (white of leek, celery, onions, fennel), roughly chopped
25g/1oz butter
150ml/¼pt white wine
juice of 1 lemon
about 1.2l/2pt water
bouquet garni (parsley or parsley stalks, thyme, bay leaves)

GAME STOCK

MAKES ABOUT 600ML/1PT

1.5kg/3lb game bones and
    trimmings
450g/1lb veal bones
25ml/1floz oil
25g/1oz tomato purée
2.5l/4½pt water
2 onions
175g/6oz leeks
2 medium carrots
3 stalks celery
2 tomatoes
50g/2oz mushrooms
4 garlic cloves
1 tsp black peppercorns
1 sprig of fresh thyme
1 sprig of fresh rosemary
2 bay leaves
175ml/6floz red wine
175ml/6floz port

The best bones and trimmings to use for this recipe are venison and hare as they give a stronger, much gamier flavour than other game bones. The further the stock is reduced at the end, the stronger in taste and richer in colour it will become. This stock, as with any other, will keep for up to 4 days in the refrigerator, or several weeks in the freezer.

Method

Chop the game bones, trimmings and the veal bones quite finely. Heat the oil in a roasting pan, add the bones and trimmings and stir well. Roast in an oven heated to 230°C/450°F/gas 8 or until a rich brown, turning them occasionally. Dot the tomato purée over the bones and return to the oven for a further 10 minutes. Drain the bones from the roasting tray, allowing as much fat as possible to run off, and transfer them to a saucepan. Cover the bones with the water and bring to the boil. As it comes to the boil skim well, then allow the stock to simmer for 15 minutes, skimming as necessary. Roughly chop all of the vegetables and add to the stock together with herbs and red wine, and simmer slowly for about 4 hours.

Strain the stock through a fine strainer or muslin. Add the port and return to the boil, skimming as necessary. Reduce until only about 600ml/1pt remains.

PHEASANT STOCK

Method

MAKES ABOUT 1.2L/2PT

1.75kg/4lb pheasant bones
1 onion
225g/8oz leeks
2 stalks celery
2 carrots
2 garlic cloves
1 tbsp oil
1 tbsp tomato purée
225ml/8floz red wine
1.7l/3pt water
600ml/1pt veal stock (see page
    201)
3 juniper berries, crushed
1 bay leaf
1 sprig of rosemary
1 sprig of thyme
½ tsp black peppercorns,
    crushed

Roughly chop the pheasant bones. Finely chop all of the vegetables and the garlic. Heat the oil in a roasting pan, add the bones, and turn them in the oil. Place in an oven heated to 230°C/450°F/gas 8 for about 20 minutes or until golden brown. Dot the tomato purée over the bones and return to the oven for a further 5 minutes. Transfer the bones to a saucepan. Pour off the fat from the roasting pan and deglaze the pan with the red wine, scraping up all the caramelized juices. Pour this over the bones, add the water and the veal stock and bring to the boil. As it comes to the boil, skim from time to time to remove any scum. Once boiling and no more scum is being thrown up, add the vegetables, herbs and peppercorns. Simmer for 1½ hours. Pour the stock through a fine sieve or muslin. Once made, the stock will keep for up to 4 days in the refrigerator or several weeks in a freezer.

VEAL STOCK

Without a good base stock, a finished sauce can never be a good one, and the one thing that a good stock needs is time. Many people only simmer their veal stock for a couple of hours; I much prefer to cook it for at least 6 hours. It is not until after 6 hours that the bones will have given up all their flavour.

MAKES 1.2L/2PT
1.5kg/3–3½lb veal bones, coarsely chopped
25g/1oz tomato purée
3l/6pt water
2 medium carrots, chopped
1 small onion, chopped
1 small leek, chopped
2 stalks celery, chopped
50g/2oz mushrooms, chopped
2 medium tomatoes, chopped
1 sprig of fresh thyme
1 sprig of fresh rosemary
½ bay leaf
225ml/8floz dry white wine

Method

Brown the bones in a roasting tray in an oven heated to 230°C/450°F/gas 8, turning from time to time. When lightly browned, dot the tomato purée over them and continue browning for a further 10 minutes. Drain the bones of any fat and transfer them to a large saucepan, then add the water and bring to the boil. Once the stock comes to the boil, lower the heat and skim – a lot of fat and scum will have risen to the surface. Allow to simmer for 5 minutes, skimming as necessary. Add the vegetables and the herbs, pour in the white wine and continue to simmer gently for 6 hours.

After 6 hours, strain the stock through muslin or a fine strainer. If there is more than 1.2l/2pt of stock, reduce it over a high heat until only this amount remains. If you do not do this, the finished stock will not have sufficient strength.

Note

Once cold, the stock should keep in the refrigerator for up to 2 weeks or, alternatively, you can freeze it for longer.

COURT BOUILLON

Court bouillon is used to cook all kinds of fish and shellfish, both for eating hot and cold. If the fish is to be eaten cold or is to be used at a later date, it is best to leave it in the court bouillon – this will prevent the fish from drying out and will also improve its flavour.

MAKES 1.5L/2½PT
2 medium onions
2 medium carrots
1 leek
2 stalks celery
¼ bulb fennel
25g/1 oz butter
50ml/2floz white wine vinegar
300ml/½pt dry white wine
1.2l/2pt water
2 stalks parsley
2 bay leaves
1 garlic clove
10g/¼oz black peppercorns
25g/1oz salt

Method

Peel and wash all the vegetables and roughly cut them up into small pieces. Melt the butter in a saucepan, add the vegetables, cover with a lid and sweat for 8–10 minutes. Pour in the vinegar, wine and water and bring to the boil. When boiling, add the herbs, garlic, peppercorns and salt and simmer for 15 minutes.

Bread Sauce

MAKES ABOUT 600ML/1PT
1 onion
2 cloves
50g/2oz fresh white bread,
    with crusts removed
15g/½oz butter
450ml/¾pt milk
50ml/2floz double cream
salt and freshly ground white
    pepper
grated nutmeg

*Bread sauce is the traditional accompaniment for grouse and all types
of roast poultry and game.*

Method
Peel the onion and cut it in half. Push the cloves into one half of the
on on and finely chop the other half. Cut the bread into cubes. Melt
the butter in a saucepan over medium heat, add the chopped onion
and sweat until soft. Pour in the milk and add the studded onion.
Bring to the boil, reduce the heat and barely simmer for 20 minutes.
Add the bread, return to the boil then cook for a further 20 minutes
over very low heat.

To Serve
Remove the half onion, stir in the cream and return to the boil.
Season to taste with the salt, pepper and nutmeg and serve.

Curry Sauce

MAKES ABOUT 1.2L/2PT
20g/¾oz butter
3 onions, sliced
1 banana, chopped
3 dessert apples, peeled, cored
    and sliced
2 tomatoes, chopped
15g/½oz sultanas
15g/½oz desiccated coconut
4 tsp tomato purée
50g/2oz curry powder
1.7l/3pt chicken stock (see
    page 198)

Method
Melt the butter in a saucepan, add the onions, cover and sweat over
medium heat until they start to soften. Add the banana and the
apples and continue cooking, covered, until they start to soften. Add
the tomatoes and continue cooking in the same way. Add the
sultanas and coconut and cook for a further minute. Stir in the
tomato purée, reduce the heat slightly and cook for a couple of
minutes, stirring to prevent burning. Stir in the curry powder and
cook for another couple of minutes, stirring occasionally. Gradually
add the stock and bring to the boil.

Either reduce the heat as far as is possible and cook for about 2
hours or, as I prefer to do, cook in a moderate oven, 180°C/350°F/
gas 4, for the same length of time, stirring occasionally. Once
cooked, press the sauce through a strainer. The sauce will keep
perfectly well in a refrigerator for a few days. Remember to keep it
covered, however, because it will quickly affect other foods in its
vicinity.

Tomato Sauce

Method

Melt the butter in a saucepan. Add the shallots, celery and leek and sweat over low heat without colouring for about 4 minutes. Add the tomatoes and continue to sweat for a further 4 minutes. Stir in the tomato purée and the remaining ingredients. Season with a little salt, bring to the boil and simmer for 25 minutes. Once cooked, pour through a fine strainer, pressing down on the vegetables to extract as much juice and flavour as possible.

MAKES 300ML/½PT

15g/½oz unsalted butter
3 shallots, roughly chopped
50g/2oz celery, roughly chopped
50g/2oz white of leek, roughly chopped
5 tomatoes, roughly chopped
2 tsp tomato purée
1 garlic clove, roughly chopped
2 tbsp white wine vinegar
300ml/½pt chicken stock (see page 198)
12 whole white peppercorns
2 sprigs of fresh tarragon
salt

Poivrade Sauce

Method

Roughly chop the game bones and trimmings. Heat the oil in a roasting pan, add the bones and coat them in the hot oil. Place in an oven heated to 230°C/450°F/gas 8 until well browned, turning them occasionally. Transfer the bones to a large saucepan. Cover with the marinade, water and veal stock. Bring to the boil, skimming as necessary, then turn the heat down to a bare simmer. Roughly chop all the vegetables, then brown them in the fat from the bones but do not allow them to get too brown as this will turn the stock bitter. Drain them from the fat and add to the stock. Add the remaining ingredients and simmer for 3 hours. Pour the stock through a fine strainer then pass it through muslin.

MAKES ABOUT 750–900ML/ 1¼–1½PT

1.75kg/4lb game bones and trimmings
50ml/2floz oil
600ml/1pt cooked marinade (see page 207)
1.25l/2¼pt water
350ml/12floz veal stock (see page 201)
2 onions
2 carrots
2 stalks celery
85g/3oz leeks
2 garlic cloves
2 tomatoes
2 sprigs of fresh thyme
2 bay leaves
2 sprigs of fresh rosemary
few parsley stalks
4 juniper berries
2 tsp black peppercorns, crushed

LOBSTER SAUCE

MAKES 1.2L/2PT
675g/1½lb lobster shells
25ml/1floz oil
225g/8oz mirepoix (leek,
    celery, carrot, onion)
½ garlic clove, crushed
85ml/3floz brandy or
    Armagnac
1½ tbsp tomato purée
1.7l/3pt fish stock (see page
    199)
1 bay leaf
1 sprig of fresh rosemary
10g/¼oz fresh tarragon
pinch of saffron

Method

Chop up the shells so that they are quite small. Heat the oil in an ovenproof pan, add the mirepoix of vegetables and the garlic, cover with a lid and sweat over a medium heat, stirring occasionally, until the vegetables start to soften. Add the lobster shells and continue to sweat for a further 10 minutes, then add the brandy and allow it to reduce by about half. Stir in the tomato purée, fish stock and herbs and bring to the boil. Continue cooking in an oven heated to 180°C/350°F/gas 4 for 1½ to 2 hours (the liquid should be just simmering). When the sauce is cooked, strain through muslin or a fine strainer.

Note

This recipe should yield at least 1.2l/2pt of finished sauce which can be used for many things. It can be served as a sauce in its own right (it is delicious with chicken) or reduced with cream to make a richer sauce. It can also be used as a base for consommé.

QUINCE JELLY

MAKES ABOUT 1.25KG/2½LB
900g/2lb quinces
2.25l/4pt water
1.25kg/2½lb sugar

The quince is a very old and often forgotten fruit, which produces the most wonderful, delicately flavoured rose pink jelly that will complement any type of game, whether it is served hot or cold. It goes well with Terrine of Grouse (see page 72).

Method

Thinly slice the quinces and place them in a large pan with the water, bring to the boil and simmer gently until the fruit is soft. Once cooked, drain the liquid off without pressing the quinces. Leave to go cold then pour the juice through a muslin-lined strainer. Dissolve the sugar in the juice and bring it to the boil, skimming as necessary. Continue boiling rapidly until the jelly is ready. To test, place a spoon of the jelly on to a cold plate – it is ready when the surface wrinkles as you draw your finger through it. Alternatively, use a jam thermometer – the jelly is cooked at 105°C/220°F. As soon as it is ready, remove it from the heat and allow to cool slightly. Warm the jars with hot water to prevent cracking then pour in the jelly. Leave to go cold, cover the surface of the jelly with waxed paper and seal the jars.

Garlic Vinaigrette

Method

Mix the garlic and shallots together in a bowl. Season, then add the wine vinegar and water. Whisk in the oils.

This will keep perfectly well in the refrigerator for up to a week and is best left to stand for at least an hour before using to allow the flavour of the garlic to permeate through the dressing.

Makes 600ml/1pt

4 garlic cloves, finely chopped
85g/3oz shallots, finely chopped
salt and freshly ground white pepper
85ml/3floz white wine vinegar
120ml/4floz water
120ml/4floz walnut oil
175ml/6floz salad oil

Tomato Vinaigrette

Method

Blanch and skin the tomatoes and roughly cut them up. Heat the olive oil in a saucepan, add the shallots and gently soften for a minute without colouring. Add the tomatoes and stir in the tomato purée, followed by the garlic and the sherry vinegar. Bring to the boil and then simmer over a very low heat for 10 minutes. Season to taste.

When cooked, allow the vinaigrette to cool and then pass it through a sieve. Do not force it through; all you want is the resulting liquid.

Note

The vinaigrette will keep perfectly well for up to 4 days if stored in a refrigerator, but allow it to come to room temperature before using; if it is too cold, it will lose some flavour.

Makes 450ml/¾pt

5 medium tomatoes
120ml/4floz olive oil
50g/2oz shallots, roughly chopped
25g/1oz tomato purée
1 small garlic clove, crushed
50ml/2floz sherry vinegar
salt and freshly ground white pepper

MARINADES

Meat is marinated for three basic reasons, to tenderize, preserve and enhance its flavour. There are two basic types of marinade – cooked and uncooked. The uncooked marinade would normally be used for small game and smaller pieces of meat, whereas the cooked marinade is used for larger cuts or joints. The length of time meat is left to marinate will obviously depend on what it is, whether a cut or a joint, and the type of marinade used. Normally an uncooked marinade is only used for a relatively short period of about 6–8 hours. A cooked marinade on the other hand will hold the meat for up to 4–5 days depending on weather conditions. My own personal preference would be to use marinades for slightly older game, or where the marinade can be added to a sauce to enhance its flavour. Although marinating does impregnate the meat with the flavours of the herbs, vegetables and wine used, I find it also sometimes detracts from the flavour of the meat.

UNCOOKED MARINADE

1 carrot, thinly sliced
1 stalk celery, thinly sliced
4 shallots, thinly sliced
1 garlic clove, roughly
   chopped
1 parsley stalk
1 sprig of fresh thyme
1 bay leaf
3 juniper berries, crushed
6 black peppercorns, crushed
½ tbsp dry white wine
4 tbsp white wine vinegar
4 tbsp oil
salt

Allow the marinade to sit for at least 1 hour before adding the meat so that the flavours have time to marry. Turn the meat from time to time.

Method
Mix all the ingredients in a shallow dish, large enough to fit the meat in one layer. Leave for 1 hour before adding meat.

COOKED MARINADE

Method

Heat the oil in a saucepan, add all vegetables and sweat over low heat until they start to soften but without colouring. Add the rest of the ingredients and bring to the boil. Reduce the heat to low and simmer for 30 minutes. Let the marinade go cold before adding the meat.

4 tbsp oil
2 carrots, thinly sliced
2 stalks celery, thinly sliced
4 shallots, thinly sliced
1 onion, thinly sliced
2 garlic cloves, roughly chopped
few parsley stalks
2 sprigs of fresh thyme
2 sprigs of fresh rosemary
1 bay leaf
3 juniper berries, crushed
6 black peppercorns, crushed
1 tbsp red wine
150ml/¼pt red wine vinegar
300ml/½pt water
salt

PANADA

Panada is used as a binding agent for mousses and forcemeats. This recipe will actually make more than is probably required but it is difficult to make it in smaller quantities than given here.

Method

Sift the flour on to a piece of folded greaseproof paper. Bring the milk to the boil in a saucepan, with the butter and a little salt and pepper. As soon as it boils tip in all of the flour and beat in over high heat. Continue beating the mixture over high heat until it comes away from the sides of the pan and makes a ball. Turn into a mixing bowl and leave to cool. When cooled, add the egg and beat in well until smooth.

50g/2oz plain flour
100ml/3½floz milk
20g/¾oz unsalted butter
salt and freshly ground white pepper
1 egg

CLARIFIED BUTTER

MAKES ABOUT 115G/7½OZ
225g/8oz butter
2 tsp water

Method

Cut the butter into small pieces and place it in a saucepan with the water. Set over very gentle heat and allow it to melt. Place the saucepan into a bain-marie and let it simmer until the butter clears, about 1 hour.

Once the butter is clear, carefully strain, through a muslin-lined strainer, being careful not to disturb the milky solids at the bottom. The butter can be stored for up to 1 week in the refrigerator.

FOIE GRAS BUTTER

4 PORTIONS
115g/4oz fresh foie gras
115g/4oz unsalted butter

This is a great way of using trimmings and off-cuts of foie gras. Once made it will keep for 3–4 weeks in the freezer. Add to a stock to make a buttery sauce, or whisk a knob into a finished sauce to give it a luxurious velvety texture.

Method

Allow the foie gras and the butter to soften slightly at room temperature, then push the foie gras through a fine sieve. Mix it well with the soft butter, making sure it is evenly incorporated. Use a sheet of greaseproof paper to roll the butter into a sausage. Either chill it well if using that day or freeze it until required. Cut it into pieces straight from the freezer – there is no need to thaw.

BRIOCHE

Brioche can be served with any pâté or terrine, but it is particularly suited to foie gras and smooth pâtés like the Chicken Liver Parfait on page 180. Serve it lightly toasted, plain or sprinkled with a little icing sugar and browned under the grill. It can, like any bread, be made into many different shapes, but it is usually cooked in a round fluted brioche tin, either one large tin or about 20 individual ones. This recipe is sufficient for a large mould.

15g/½oz fresh yeast
85ml/3floz milk
25g/1oz sugar
450g/1lb strong plain white
    flour
5 eggs
2 tsp salt
275g/10oz unsalted butter,
    softened
1 egg yolk beaten with 1 tbsp
    milk

Method

Cream the yeast, milk and sugar together. Add the flour, the eggs, and the salt and knead it all together until smooth. Gradually add the softened butter and continue kneading until the dough is smooth, glossy and elastic. Cover the bowl and leave it to stand in a warm place for 2–3 hours or until the dough has doubled in size. Once proved, turn the dough two or three times in a bowl, cover again and chill for 4 and up to 12 hours so that the butter firms up. Place the dough in the tin and leave it to prove again at toom temperature until it has almost doubled in size.

To Cook

Lightly brush the top of the brioche with the egg wash. Bake in an oven heated to 220°C/425°F/gas 7 for 35–40 minutes. Turn the brioche out of the tin on to a wire rack to cool.

RAVIOLI/NOODLE PASTE

Method

Sieve together the flour and the salt. Knead in the egg and the oil, then add sufficient water to make a dough without it being too sticky or too dry. Mix in well to make a smooth paste.

Cover with a damp cloth and leave to rest in a refrigerator for at least 2 hours before using.

MAKES 350G/12 OZ
350g/12oz strong plain flour
pinch of salt
1 egg
50ml/2floz oil

Puff Pastry

Makes about 1.25kg/2¾lb
450g/1lb cold unsalted butter
450g/1lb plain flour
2 tsp salt
225ml/8floz cold water

Method

Gently melt 50g/2oz of the butter. Sift the flour on to the work surface and form into a mound. Make a well in the centre. Dissolve the salt in the water and pour into the well, then pour in the melted, but not hot, butter. Gradually mix together the flour and water mixture using your fingertips. When thoroughly mixed, knead the dough with the palms of your hands until completely smooth. Wrap the dough in greaseproof paper and leave to rest in the refrigerator for at least 2 hours.

Dust the work surface with a little flour and roll out the dough to form four flaps of about 10cm/4 inches wide, each at right angles to one another, and leaving a thick piece of dough in the middle. Knead the remaining butter to form one supple slab; it must still be cold as well as supple. Place this in the centre of the dough. Fold over each of the flaps to completely enclose the butter. Return to the refrigerator, covered, for a further 30 minutes.

Again, lightly flour the work surface and gently roll the dough into a 60×40cm/24×16 inch rectangle. Keep the surface of the table dusted with flour while rolling and always roll the pastry away from yourself. Mark the rectangle into three sections. First fold one end over the middle section and then fold the final section over the other. This is called a 'turn'. At all times try to keep the edges and the corners of the dough straight. If they are not then the pastry will not rise evenly when cooking.

Now turn the dough through 90 degrees and roll it out again into a rectangle as before, flouring the work surface as you go. Once again, mark out three equal sections and fold over as before. The pastry has now had two 'turns'. Cover the pastry and leave to rest and firm up again in the refrigerator for at least 30 minutes. It is important not to allow the pastry to become too warm when working it. On a hot day it may be best to keep returning it to the refrigerator after each single turn to prevent the butter starting to melt. Give the pastry another two 'turns' exactly as the first two, cover and return to the refrigerator for another 30 minutes. Give the pastry two final 'turns' so that it has now had six 'turns' in total. After resting for a further 30 minutes, the pastry will be ready for use. It will last for about 4 days in the refrigerator or, if you wish, freeze it and then you can keep it for a few weeks.

Shortcrust Pastry

This light, crumbly pastry is mainly used for flans and tartlets and will keep in the refrigerator for 4–5 days. If required, water can be substituted for the milk. The amount of liquid needed will depend on the flour used – the better the flour, the more liquid.

Makes about 350g/12oz
225g/8oz plain flour
1 tsp salt
150g/5oz unsalted butter
1 egg
25–50ml/1–2floz cold milk

Method

Sift the flour and salt together, then rub the butter and the flour together with your fingertips. Add the egg and milk and mix together. When they are mixed in, knead the pastry into a smooth dough, but do not overwork – the finished dough should be quite firm. Wrap in greaseproof paper or put in a polythene bag and store in the refrigerator. Allow to rest for at least 1 hour before using.

Filo Pastry

You can buy ready-made filo pastry from Greek or Turkish delicatessens and I must admit that it is very good, probably better than I or this recipe will make. The problem with filo pastry is getting it thin enough – if it is too thick it is inedible.

Makes about 175g/6oz
85g/3oz strong plain flour
25g/1oz cornflour
pinch of salt
2 tsp oil
50ml/2floz cold water

Method

Sift the flour, cornflour and salt together. Make a well in the centre and add the oil and about half of the water. Mix into the flour and continue adding more water until the dough is smooth and does not stick to your hands. The dough should then be covered with a damp cloth and left to rest in the refrigerator for a minimum of 2 hours. (The paste will not be elastic enough if left for a shorter period.) I prefer to leave the paste for a longer period, and find 24 hours about right. It will keep for up to 2 days in the refrigerator, as long as it is covered with a damp cloth.

To use, roll out the pastry as far as you can, using plenty of flour on the work surface at all times. When you have rolled it out as thin as possible, place the sheet over the backs of your hands and gently pull downwards, stretching all the time, until you can virtually see through it. Once rolled out, the pastry should be used straightaway.

PREPARING AND COOKING POULTRY AND GAME

The art of cooking, for that is what it is, requires a love of food in all its forms, but before you can realistically hope to produce a good dish or become a good cook there are certain basic principles you must learn. The term cooking is not confined to that process whereby heat is applied to raw food, it applies to all its aspects, from buying to preparing, through the actual cooking and finally to serving. If the basic food is badly prepared or the wrong method of cooking used or badly applied, then the dish in question will never be great, probably not even good. It is therefore essential that you read this chapter whether you already know what you are doing, to refresh your memory, or are considering a new technique. Even as an experienced chef, I am still learning about food and will continually learn; no one person knows it all, we all learn from one another. Without knowledge of the basics, no-one can hope to become a successful cook.

PREPARING POULTRY AND GAME

The preparation, especially of game, is probably the most disconcerting part of a recipe for the majority of people. 'What in the world am I supposed to do with this pheasant our neighbour has just given me – it still has its feathers on!'

Worry not, help is at hand. In this section, I have given some easy-to-follow step-by-step instructions along with diagrams for just that sort of occasion. From plucking to trussing, from skinning to jointing, they are all, I hope, clearly explained.

Of course, the amount of preparation you have to do will be greatly reduced if you are buying from a butcher or supermarket as it will already have been prepared for you. If this is the case, make sure you get the neck and livers if it is a bird, and the trimmings and bones if it is a rabbit or hare, for instance. Even if you do not require them for the particular recipe you are about to tackle, they will keep in the freezer until needed. Even when buying a pre-prepared bird, you should always singe it before using, since this is not something that is always done by the supplier. Singeing gets rid of the fine hairs that remain after plucking, and which cooking will not remove.

Plucking and Singeing

1. *Hold the bird in one hand, breast up and head away.*

2. *Using your free hand, grasp a few feathers and giving a sharp tug towards the head pull out the feathers, being careful not to damage the skin in the process.*

3. *Work your way back along the breasts, then the legs. Remove all the feathers in this way. The tail and wing feathers are tougher than the others and have to be removed one at a time.*

4. *Singe the plucked bird by passing it over an open flame, to remove the covering of fine hairs that remain.*

DRAWING

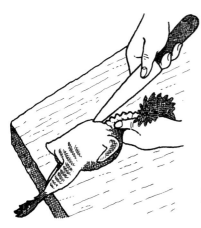

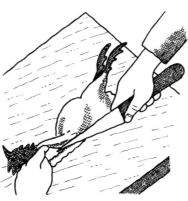

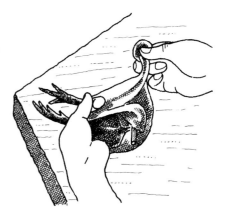

1. Lay the bird on its breasts, pinch the flesh under the neck and make an incision from the base of the neck to two-thirds of the way towards the head.

2. Turn the bird on to its back, insert the point of the knife above the neck bone at its base and cut through. Cut off the head.

3. Pull the crop away from the skin around the neck.

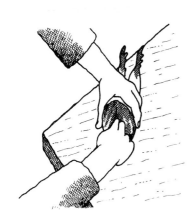

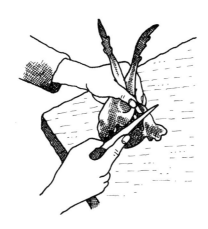

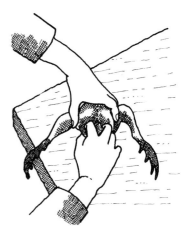

4. Insert your fore and middle fingers and ease the lungs away from the back bone, and free the windpipe and gullet.

5. Make a slit above the vent.

6. Insert your fore and middle fingers into the slit, hook them around the stomach and pull out the entrails. Cut around the vent to remove.

Preparing Suprêmes

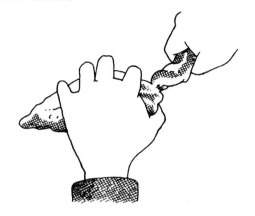

1. *Hold the bird aloft by one wing. Using a sharp knife, cut around the base of the wing as close to the breast as is possible. Repeat on the other wing.*

2. *Holding the bird steady with one hand, twist the wing against the joint and pull it off.*

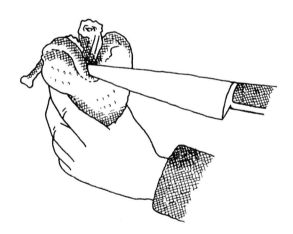

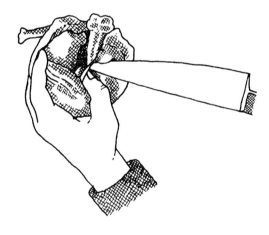

3. *Insert the point of the knife into the neck of the bird, pivoting the point on the neck bone. Twist the knife on its point, scraping it against the wish bone on both sides.*

4. *Separate the wish bone from the flesh with your fingers and cut off the bone at the base, then pull it out.*

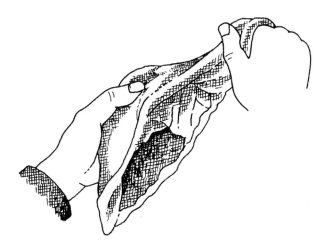

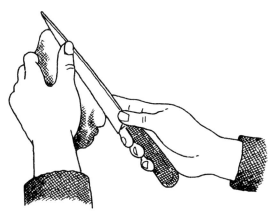

5. *Pull the skin away from the breasts and back.*

6. *Holding the bird in your left hand and, using a sharp knife, cut down one side of the breast bone.*

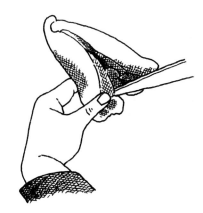

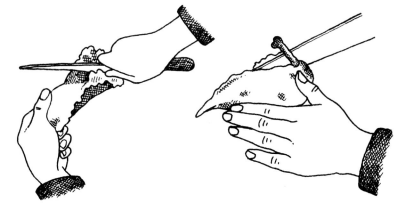

7. *Run the knife down the side of the carcass against the bone and cut through the wing joint.*

8. *Turn the bird on its side and pull the suprême off.*

9. *Trim away any excess fat from around the suprême.*

TRUSSING A BIRD FOR ROASTING: METHOD 1

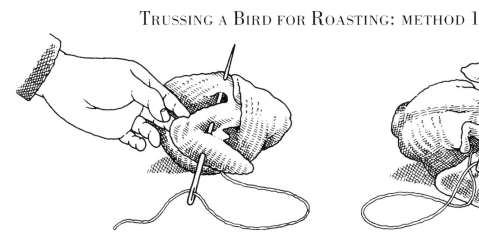

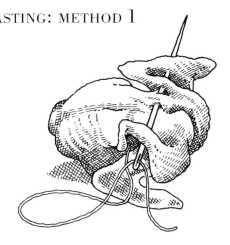

1. With the bird on its back, push the needle through between the two bones of the first part of the wing, over the bone on the next part and through the skin on the back.

2. Push the needle through the neck flap, then repeat the process in reverse order for the other wing. Pull the string through.

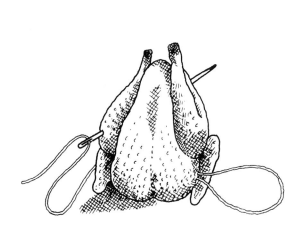

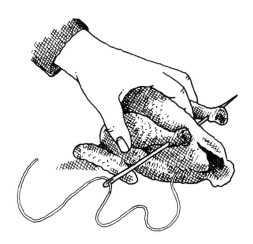

3. Turn the bird on to its back and push the trussing needle through the leg close to the joint at a 45 degree angle, coming out at the parson's nose end of the carcass on the opposite side of entry.

4. Pass the needle through the skin under the bone as close as possible to the top joint of the leg, pass the needle under the point of the breast bone and through the opposite leg.

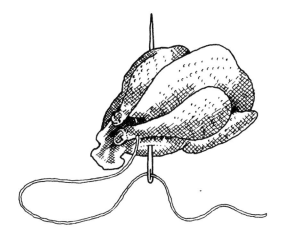

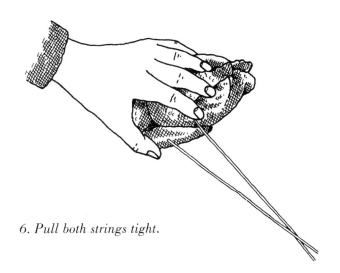

5. Push the needle through the carcass underneath the top leg joint at a 45 degree angle to come out beside the middle joint of the opposite leg.

6. Pull both strings tight.

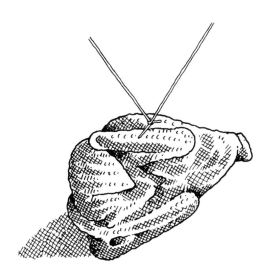

7. Tie the string.

TRUSSING A BIRD FOR ROASTING: METHOD 2

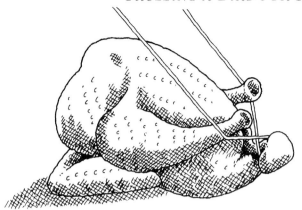

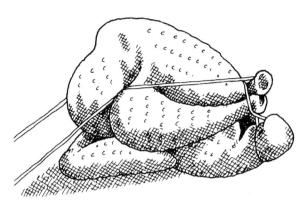

1. Pass the string under the parson's nose, then cross it over the top. Bring the string up both sides of the legs and cross it over.

2. Pull the string tightly down between the legs and the breasts.

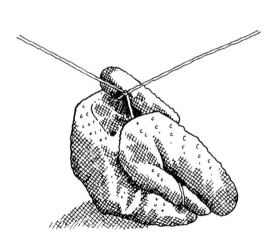

3. Bring the string over the top side of the wing bone and under the bird.

4. Tie the string off.

SKINNING A RABBIT OR HARE

 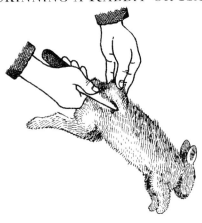 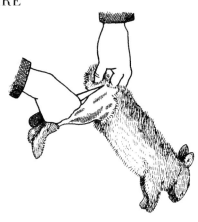

1. *Cut through the skin at the base of each leg.*

2. *Cut the skin along the inside of the hind legs down to the belly and free the skin.*

3. *Cut through the tail.*

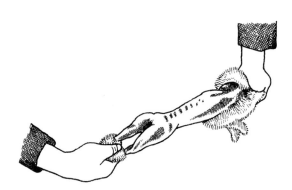

4. *Holding the animal firmly by the back legs, pull off the skin towards the head using your free hand. Chop off the head.*

Jointing a Rabbit or Hare

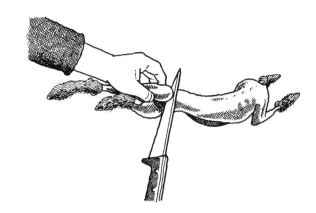

1. *Make an incision along the belly and remove the innards.*

2. *At the base of the spine is a 'V'-shaped bone (the pelvis). Cut through the meat on the leg side of this bone down to the spine.*

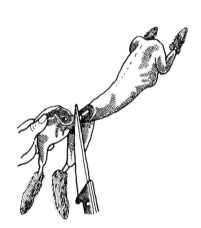

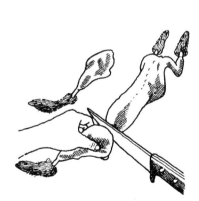

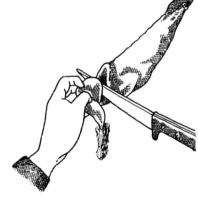

3. *Cut through the leg joint and remove the leg.*

4. *Repeat on the other leg. Chop off the feet.*

5. *Cut off the front legs and chop off the feet.*

222

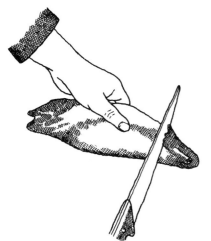

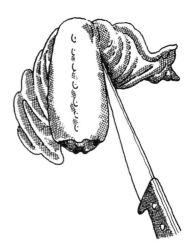

6. *Chop off the end of the carcass on the saddle side of the pelvic bone.*

7. *Chop off the neck from the saddle.*

8. *Cut away the belly flap.*

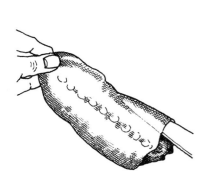

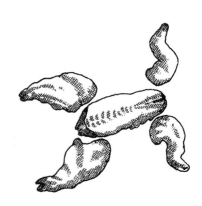

9. *Slide the knife under the sinew.*

10. *Cut away the sinew.*

11. *The finished joints.*

COOKING POULTRY AND GAME

The most important point to remember when cooking any food is not to overcook it. There is a point in all foods when they are cooked to perfection, a little under and it would be considered raw, a little over and it will become tasteless and dry. Both poultry and game are prone to dryness. This is basically because they contain very little fat, unlike beef or pork for, instance, which are reared to contain an expected quantity of fat. Game especially, because it is not farmed but wild, carries very little fat. Always keep the meat a little pink even if you prefer it more well done, you will find the flavour is vastly improved. How many times have you cooked a chicken or turkey and said 'isn't this tender' because the meat falls off the bone. It is not tender, it is annihilated, cooked so long it has started to disintegrate.

All the cooking times I have given throughout the book work for me, although there are a few variables that must be taken in consideration. For instance, how efficient is your oven? If the thermostat is not working correctly then this will affect the cooking time. Fierceness of hob heat will make a difference to searing – was it enough or even too much? Please, use the cooking times as a guide and not as if they were written on tablets of stone.

Poaching

To poach means to partly or fully cover in liquid, preferably stock, which is then heated gently until it just starts to tremble. The liquid is then held at this point until the meat is cooked. I find it best to transfer the pan to the oven to complete the cooking process; this will prevent the liquid from boiling. If the poaching medium is allowed to boil, it will make the meat tough and shrink. When poaching, it is important to use a pan or container just large enough to take the pieces of meat without them touching or overlapping each other. If you do not have a pan large enough, then use two rather than the same one twice.

Steaming

Steaming is an alternative to poaching, retaining more of the natural flavour, moisture and nutrients of the food. It needs nothing adding to it to enable it to be cooked, and is, therefore, better suited to the calorie conscious. It is a method well suited to chicken, pheasant, quail and guinea fowl, but not recommended for furred game or large cuts of meat.

The food to be steamed is put in a perforated container over a pan of boiling water or stock so that the steam produced by the boiling liquid envelops it. Steaming is a quick and clean method of cooking that was, until quite recently, much maligned in the West as being fit only for invalids. It is important when steaming not to allow the food to come in contact with the boiling liquid, to keep the liquid constantly boiling, and not to allow the pan to boil dry.

Grilling

Grilling is suitable for all poultry and game when cooking in portion-sized pieces but not for large cuts or whole birds. There are two forms of grilling: over heat on a charcoal grill or barbecue, or under a grill giving top heat only. Always preheat the grill to its highest setting first so that the meat sears quickly thus entrapping its juices – the heat can always be turned down afterwards. Remember also when grilling, that the meat will need basting from time to time.

Shallow Frying or Sautéeing

This method is often called pan-frying and differs from deep-frying in that only a small quantity of fat or oil is needed. In fact, since the arrival of non-stick frying pans, most foods can be sautéed dry. When using fat to fry in, a combination of oil and butter is best: the butter gives it flavour and the oil will prevent the butter from burning too quickly. If you want to use only butter, use clarified butter (see page 208): this will not burn, whereas normal butter will. The food should always be started in a very hot pan to sear the outside, then the heat is reduced to finish cooking gently.

Braising

Braising is a method of cooking in the oven, normally on a bed of vegetables with the addition of stock or wine. Braising is a slow method of cooking and is always carried out in a covered pan in a moderate oven. The meat should be basted occasionally with the cooking liquor and the finished dish is normally served with a sauce made from its juices. Especially suited to large cuts of meat or whole birds, it is good for older and furred game.

Roasting

This is probably the method most people associate with both game and poultry. It is essential to use a very hot oven to begin with, then if necessary reduce the heat later. Always sear the meat or bird well on all sides on top of the stove before committing it to the oven. The meat will need basting with its juices from time to time to prevent it drying out and burning. Before roasting whole birds, always season them inside the cavity as well as out. The addition of a few sprigs of fresh rosemary or thyme to the cavity before roasting will enhance the flavour of the meat.

GLOSSARY

Bain-marie

A bath of warm water rather like a double saucepan into which a saucepan of sauce is placed to keep warm or to prevent it from boiling and spoiling.

Bard

To cover the breasts of a bird, usually game, with a thin layer of fat or bacon tied on with string, which bastes the breast meat as it cooks and prevents it from drying out.

Baste

To keep the meat moist by occasionally spooning the cooking juices over it during cooking, braising or roasting.

Blanch

To lightly cook vegetables ready for further cooking and to heighten colour. Certain vegetables, such as tomatoes, are blanched before peeling – the skins come off more easily.

Caul

The fatty, net-like lining of a pig's stomach. It is used for wrapping lean meats before cooking; the caul melts and bastes the meat during cooking.

Clarify

To remove all suspended solids from a liquid to create a clear soup or consommé. Also used to describe the process of removing all solids and liquid from butter to stop it from burning.

Consommé

A strong stock which has been clarified with egg white to produce a clear soup.

Court bouillon

A strong stock for poaching all types of fish and shellfish as well as some meats (see page 201 for recipe).

Crushed ice

Crushed ice is preferred as it has a greater surface area than cubed ice and therefore more chilling power. To make, wrap cubed ice in a cloth and beat with a rolling pin.

Draw

Used to describe the removal of a bird's innards (see page 215).

Escalope

Meat, fish or poultry cut on a slant, giving it a larger surface area.

Foie gras

Fattened liver of duck or goose; a great delicacy.

Julienne

The term used for cutting vegetables into fine strips, no more than 4cm/1½inches long. Normally used for garnishing.

Lard

To insert strips of fat into meat using a larding needle. This moistens very lean meat such as venison, hare or boar.

Marinade

A liquid made from wine, herbs, vinegar and vegetables, in which pieces of meat are soaked to improve their flavour, and tenderize and moisten it.

Marinate

To soak pieces of meat in a marinade (see pages 206–7).

Medallion

A medallion, or *médaillon*, is meat or vegetables cut or formed into rounds the size and shape of a medallion.

Mirepoix

Roughly chopped vegetables used in stocks and sauces, to be strained out and discarded before serving.

Papillote

An envelope made from either paper or foil to contain fish or meat, which is then tightly sealed and baked. The cooked dish is then normally served still in its envelope.

Pick

To remove the leaves of herbs from their stalks for garnishing or chopping. Also to remove any yellowing or spoilt leaves.

Reduce

To boil a liquid rapidly over high heat to concentrate the flavour by means of evaporation. Also to reduce a sauce to reach the desired consistency.

Refresh

To plunge food, normally vegetables, into cold or iced water to instantly halt the cooking process, preventing further cooking by retained heat, and to preserve and heighten their colours. They are then gently reheated just before serving.

Sear

Searing is done over high heat, normally in a frying pan or roasting tin. The pan is heated until very hot with a little oil, butter or both, and the meat is browned well on all sides briefly before being transferred to a preheated oven. This reduces cooking time and helps keep in the meat juices.

Singe

Once plucked and before being drawn (see page 215), all birds should be singed. This removes the stubble, feather ends and the down from the skin, which plucking alone will not remove. Hold the bird over a naked flame by its feet and neck and pass the bird over the flame on all sides (see page 214).

Skim

All stocks and sauces should be skimmed, using a ladle, to remove any scum that rises to the surface during cooking. Skimming is vital; without it, the stock or sauce will become cloudy as the scum cooks back into the liquid.

Suprême

Primarily associated with poultry or feathered game, the suprême is the breast and wing of a bird removed while raw, then cooked. Quite literally the best piece.

Sweat

To soften vegetables in butter, normally for soups and sauces. It must be done in a pan with a tight fitting lid over low to medium heat.

Terrine

The word terrine describes the china or earthenware dish in which meat, fish or vegetables are cooked. It has come to mean either a way of cooking or a type of food. A terrine is made from a mixture of ingredients, and is normally served cold.

Truss

To retain a pleasing shape to the bird and to prevent distortion during cooking. The legs and wings are drawn tight against the bird with string (see pages 218–20)

Turn

To shape vegetables with a sharp knife into small barrel or olive shapes for garnishing.

Zest

The rind of any citrus fruit with the white pith removed. It is normally grated or cut into fine strips.

INDEX

WITH SPECIAL THANKS TO

Neil and Frances Smith of Park Hill Produce, Appledore, Kent, for their invaluable technical knowledge and superior produce, especially their quail.

Ian Woodhouse of T.S.J. Woodhouse for coming to my rescue and supplying the majority of the meats used in this book.

Paul Cockerton of Hyams and Cockerton for supplying many of the vegetables and fruits used.

Eric Burchell and Deborah Dunn for giving me the apportunity to shoot some of the supplies myself, and for a perfectly trained cocker.

Martin Brigdale, Andrea Lampton and Gus for a job well done, and I hope we get to work together again.

The team at Macdonald for their patience with me.

Siri, Svava and Bennie for introducing us to the delights of Iceland.

But most of all to my wife, Jane, and my parents for putting up with me experimenting on them so often.